P9-CQF-507

MEAT & POTATOES

Home-cooked Favorites from Perfect Pot Roast to Chocolate Cream Pie

JUDITH CHOATE

PHOTOGRAPHY BY DAN WILBY

FOOD STYLING BY KATRINA MESAROVICH
PROP STYLING BY LYNNE MC MAHILL

SIMON & SCHUSTER
London   Sydney   New York   Tokyo   Toronto   Singapore

A KENAN BOOK

Copyright © 1992 Kenan Books, Inc.
Text copyright © Judith Choate

All rights reserved including the right of reproduction
in whole or part in any form.

Simon & Schuster
Simon & Schuster Building
Rockefeller Center
1230 Avenue of the Americas
New York, New York 10020

SIMON & SCHUSTER and colophon are registered
trademarks of Simon & Schuster, Inc.

MEAT & POTATOES
was prepared and produced by
Kenan Books, Inc.
15 West 26th Street
New York, New York 10010

Editor: Sharon Kalman
Art Director: Robert W. Kosturko
Designer: Edward Noriega
Photo Editor: Anne K. Price
Production: Karen L. Greenberg
Photographs © 1991 by Dan Wilby

1   3   5   7   9   10   8   6   4   2

Library of Congress Cataloging-in-Publication Data Available

Typeset by Bookworks Plus
Color separation by United South Sea Graphic Art Co., Ltd.
Printed and bound in Hong Kong by Leefung-Asco Printers, Ltd.

DEDICATION

So that she may never have to hear,
"That's not the way mom did it,"
I dedicate this, with love, to
Torryne, my first daughter-in-law.

TABLE OF CONTENTS

FOR GENERATIONS, YOUNG WOMEN entered marriage with a handwritten notebook carrying their family's kitchen traditions, as well as the basic information necessary to run a well-organized home. But, by the 1950s, as women began to move into the job market and not immediately into marriage, and kitchen traditions were replaced by Duncan Hines and Campbell's, these handed-down treasures were lost to most of us. *Meat and Potatoes* is my compilation of these nearly forgotten culinary gems.

Fortunately, we never strayed far from many of the home-cooked foods of the past. Meat loafs, pot roasts, meatballs and spaghetti, peas and carrots, baking powder biscuits, and chocolate cupcakes remained constants in our diet. However, in recent times they most often came, either totally or in part, from prepared mixes and cans. We quickly forgot how to make the table basics that had been perfected by previous generations of cooks.

Today, as our tastes broaden and international foodstuffs become commonplace, old-fashioned home cooking has become an exotic tradition. Simple, straightforward food that nourishes the body and the soul is now considered special, and is, once again, in demand. World-renowned chefs are bringing their mothers into their restaurant kitchens to teach them the essence of bourgeois cuisine. The foods of our agricultural past are becoming menu stars. This book makes this heritage a part of your kitchen. Just the basics, gathered together, on which you can build a family notebook of your own.

All of the recipes included are true classics taken directly from the kitchens of my grandmothers, aunts, and mother, as well as from my own. I have, however, updated some of the recipes to take advantage of the conveniences of today's home kitchen, as well as the variety of foodstuffs available to the home cook.

These are foods you will want to cook every day. Each dish can also star when you are entertaining and will especially thrill guests who are frequent restaurant diners or do not cook themselves. Memories of good old-fashioned home cooking serve as a remarkable equalizer, as each of us can recall some very special meal that came from our mother's kitchen. Everyday foods are frequently more stimulating than those experienced in the once-in-a-lifetime fine French meal.

Among my hand-me-down cookbooks, recipe files, and kitchen notebooks I recently found an unknown cook's admonition: "Just follow a few simple rules if you want to be known as a good cook. Never use anything but the finest ingredients. Use butter; unsalted is best. Fresh oils and garden-picked herbs will only make your meals better. Serve vegetables and fruits in season. Make bread at home. Stock your kitchen with country ham and real farm cheeses. Don't bother with frozen meats—make any extra meat into stews and casseroles and then freeze. Cook everything with love and serve immediately." This note, stuck in a church club's cookbook dated 1949, quite simply states what I believe is the heart of cooking meat and potatoes and other kitchen classics. This is the way my grandmother cooked for my mother, who in turn taught me to love the time I spent preparing my family's meals. I hope that I have passed the joy of cooking on to my children and that this recipe file captures the pleasures of creating kitchen classics for you.

NOTE: An asterisk indicates that the recipe is included elsewhere in the book.

The Perfect Roast Turkey with
Mickey's Stuffing

The Perfect Roast Chicken

Roast Beef and
Yorkshire Pudding

Stuffed Roast Pork

Brisket

Roast Leg of Lamb with
Spring Vegetables

Two Kinds of Ham

Roast Loin of Veal

Mixed Grill

London Broil

The Perfect Steak

The Perfect Hamburger
and Its Variations

Meat Loaf and Its Variations

My Famous Fried Chicken

Auntie's Fried Chicken

Barbecued Spareribs

1

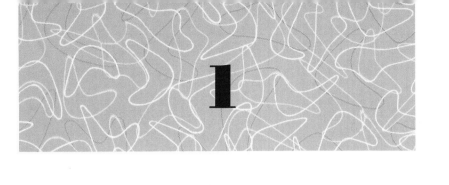

MEATS

AND

POULTRY

THE PERFECT ROAST TURKEY WITH MICKEY'S STUFFING

■

Serves 8 to 10.

1   large lemon
1   16-pound fresh turkey
      Mickey's Stuffing*
      Coarse salt to taste
      Pepper to taste
1¼ cups cold water
3   tablespoons cornstarch

■ *Preheat oven to 500°F.*

RINSE TURKEY UNDER COOL RUNNING water. Drain well and pat dry. Cut lemon in half and squeeze juice directly on turkey. Rub juice into the skin to cover entire turkey.

Remove giblets and neck and place them in a heavy saucepan with water to cover over medium-high heat. Bring to a boil. When boiling, lower heat to a simmer and simmer for about 1½ hours or until giblets are very soft, adding water as necessary.

You will need at least 2 cups giblet broth for gravy. When giblets are soft, drain off liquid. Trim off gristle and skin from giblets and neck. Finely chop giblets and neck meat. Set aside.

Place Mickey's Stuffing in neck cavity and fold skin underneath bird. Fasten with a small skewer, if desired. Place remaining stuffing in body cavity. Close the opening with small skewers or by sewing with heavy thread. Fold wing tips under wings.

Place turkey on rack in roasting pan. Push legs back against body and tie them together using heavy thread. Sprinkle turkey with coarse salt and pepper. Pour 1 cup cold water into roasting pan and enclose the entire pan with heavy-duty aluminum foil. Place in preheated oven and roast for 45 minutes. Lower heat to 375°F and continue to cook for about 2½ hours or until thigh meat is soft to the touch and juices run clear (or food thermometer registers 185°F). If after removing foil, turkey is not golden-brown, return to oven without foil for about

15 minutes or until browned. Remove from oven and place on carving board. Let stand for 15 minutes.

While turkey is resting, make gravy. Pour off and reserve all but ¼ cup fat from roasting pan. Dissolve cornstarch in remaining cold water and stir into fat. Add 2 cups giblet stock and place roasting pan on top of the stove over medium heat. Cook, stirring constantly, scraping up brown bits from the pan as you stir, for about 5 minutes or until gravy is thick. If gravy is too thick, add additional stock (or milk or water, if desired). Check the reserved pan drippings. If fat has separated from solids, pour it off and add solids to gravy for additional flavor. Pour into gravy boat.

Carve turkey as directed on page 15. However, since turkey parts are quite large, you can also slice the meat from the thighs and legs. Arrange on a serving platter and keep warm. Remove stuffing from cavities and place in separate serving bowl. Serve immediately.

MICKEY'S STUFFING

*Makes 12 cups; enough for
16-pound turkey.*

EACH THANKSGIVING I THREATEN MY son, Mickey, with a different stuffing. Threaten is all I ever do, because his dismay at not having his favorite apricot stuffing always softens his mother's heart. However, this basic stuffing can serve as your point of experimentation if you don't have such family traditions to uphold. Any dried fruit or combination of dried fruits can replace the apricots. Any nut can replace the walnuts. Corn bread crumbs can be used in place of bread cubes or in combination with them. Cooked rice, wild rice, or other grain may also serve as the basis for poultry stuffing.

12	cups dried white and whole-wheat bread cubes
½	cup unsalted butter
1	cup diced onion
¼	cup finely diced celery
1	tablespoon minced fresh parsley
1	cup walnut pieces
1½	cups diced dried apricots
2	cups warm poultry stock or water
1	tablespoon poultry seasoning
1	teaspoon chopped fresh sage (or to taste)
1	teaspoon chopped fresh thyme (or to taste)
1	teaspoon chopped fresh marjoram (or to taste)
	Salt to taste
	Pepper to taste

PLACE BREAD CUBES IN LARGE MIXING bowl. Melt butter in a heavy sauté pan over medium-high heat. When melted, add onions, celery, and parsley. Lower heat and sauté for about 10 minutes or until vegetables are very soft but not brown. Add walnuts and apricots and continue to sauté for 5 minutes. Add ½ cup stock and remaining ingredients. Stir until well combined. Toss into bread cubes. When blended, add enough warm stock or water to make a very moist but not wet mixture. Cover and refrigerate until ready to use.

NOTE: Never stuff poultry in advance of roasting because, even if refrigerated, bacteria can form quickly. Always stuff poultry just before ready to bake.

VARIATION:
One cup chopped cooked poultry livers, 1½ cups crumbled cooked sausage, or 1½ cups raw oysters may be added to this recipe in place of dried fruit and nuts.

THE PERFECT ROAST CHICKEN

━━━

Serves 4 to 6.

1   whole 6-pound roasting chicken (free-range preferred)
1   lemon
1   large onion, peeled (or 1 large orange or apple, unpeeled)
½   sprig fresh rosemary (optional)
    Coarse salt to taste
    Pepper to taste
½   cup white wine or water
1   tablespoon cornstarch (optional)
1   tablespoon cold water (optional)
1   cup chicken broth (or more as needed, optional)

■ *Preheat oven to 500°F.*

RINSE CHICKEN UNDER COOL RUNNING water. Drain well and pat dry. Reserve giblets for another use.

Cut lemon in half and squeeze juice directly on chicken. Rub juice into the skin to cover entire chicken. Place onion (or fruit) in cavity with rosemary. Fasten neck skin under chicken with a small skewer. Close cavity with skewers or by sewing with heavy thread. Fold wing tips under wings.

Place chicken on rack in a roasting pan. Push legs back against the body and tie them together using heavy thread. Sprinkle chicken with salt and pepper. Pour wine into roasting pan and place in preheated oven. Roast for 30 minutes, then lower heat to 350°F and continue to cook for about 1 hour or until chicken is golden-brown and thigh meat is soft and juices run clear.

Remove from oven and let stand for 5 minutes. Carve and serve with gravy on the side, if desired.

NOTE: If gravy is desired, place roasting pan on top of stove over medium heat. Combine cornstarch and water and stir into pan juices along with chicken broth. Bring to a boil and cook, stirring constantly, for about 3 minutes or until gravy is smooth and starch taste has cooked out. Remove from pan and add salt and pepper to taste. Serve hot.

TO CARVE POULTRY

TO REMOVE WINGS, SLICE AT JOINT from against the body. Set aside. Pull legs slightly away from body. Slice down through thigh joint to separate entire leg from body. Slice through leg joint to divide drumstick from thigh. With knife parallel to breast bone, slice breast meat away from carcass by cutting from the center of the breast slightly to the front, removing the meat in thin slices. If desired, you can gently remove skin before slicing.

The Perfect Roast Chicken garnished with orange slices and fresh rosemary.

ROAST BEEF AND YORKSHIRE PUDDING

Serves 4 to 6.

1   3-rib standing beef rib roast
    Coarse salt to taste
    Pepper to taste
    Yorkshire Pudding Batter*
3   tablespoons cornstarch or all-
    purpose flour (optional)
2   cups beef stock (or water, or half
    stock and water, optional)

■ *Preheat oven to 500°F.*

GENEROUSLY COAT RIB ROAST WITH coarse salt and pepper. Place on rack in a roasting pan, fat side up, in preheated oven. Roast for 30 minutes. Lower heat to 375°F and roast for about 15 minutes per pound for rare, 18 minutes per pound for medium, 22 minutes per pound for well done (or until meat thermometer registers 140°F for rare, 160°F for medium, or 170°F for well done).

When roast beef is done, remove from oven and let stand for 20 minutes in a warm spot to allow meat to set before carving. Do not turn the oven off if making Yorkshire Pudding.

YORKSHIRE PUDDING BATTER

Makes one 8-inch by 11-inch pan.

1½ cups all-purpose flour
¼   teaspoon baking powder
½   teaspoon salt (or to taste)
¼   teaspoon sugar
2   large eggs
1¼ cups milk

PROCESS ALL INGREDIENTS IN A blender until well combined. Allow to rest 30 minutes before pouring into hot pan.

Raise oven temperature to 425°F. Pour off 3 tablespoons beef pan drippings into an 8-inch by 11-inch pan. Place pan in preheated oven for 2 minutes or until very hot. Remove from oven. Pour Yorkshire Pudding Batter into hot pan. Return to oven and bake for about 20 minutes or until puffed and golden-brown. Cut into squares and serve immediately with roast beef.

NOTE: If you wish to make Yorkshire Pudding without roast beef, melt 3 tablespoons unsalted butter in an 8-inch by 11-inch pan and bake as directed. You may also use Yorkshire Pudding Batter to make popovers.

TO CARVE ROAST BEEF

LAY ROAST ON ITS SIDE. USING A long carving knife, carve meat away from the backbone and ribs. Stand the meat up, and holding it steady with a carving fork, use a carving knife to slice off thin pieces, cutting down across the grain. Serve immediately.

If gravy is desired, drain off all but 3 tablespoons fat from roasting pan. Place roasting pan over medium heat on top of stove. Stir in 3 tablespoons cornstarch or all-purpose flour. When well blended, whisk in beef stock (or water) and cook, stirring constantly, for about 5 minutes or until gravy is thick. Taste and adjust seasoning. Serve immediately.

NOTE: If eating family-style, the rib bones may be offered. For formal dinners, rib bones should be reserved for another use.

STUFFED ROAST PORK

━━

Serves 6 to 8.

1   5-pound tenderloin of pork
2   cups chopped dried apricots
½   cup yellow raisins
½   cup chopped water chestnuts
½   cup chopped pecans
1½ cups Calvados
½   cup white wine
3   tablespoons unsalted butter
1¼ cups diced red onion
    Salt to taste
    Pepper to taste

WIPE TENDERLOIN WITH DAMP CLOTH. Using a sharp knife (or a reamer), make a 1¼-inch diameter hole down the center of the meat. Cover and refrigerate until ready to stuff.

Combine apricots, raisins, water chestnuts, pecans, Calvados, and white wine in a nonreactive bowl. Cover and allow to marinate for 1 hour.

Melt butter in a medium-sized sauté pan over medium-high heat. When melted, add onions and cook, stirring frequently, for about 15 minutes or until onions brown and begin to caramelize. Add apricot mixture and stir to combine. Remove from heat. Cover and let stand for 30 minutes. Then drain off and reserve any remaining liquid.

■ *Preheat oven to 450°F.*

Stuff apricot mixture into the center hole of the tenderloin. Rub outside of loin with remaining liquid and season with salt and pepper. Place on rack in roasting pan in preheated oven. Roast for 15 minutes. Lower heat to 375°F and cook for about 2 hours or until a meat thermometer registers 185°F. Remove from oven and let stand 5 minutes. Cut ¼-inch slices and drizzle with any pan juices. Serve immediately.

BRISKET

━━

Serves 6.

4   cups thinly sliced onions
1   3-pound brisket of beef, well
    trimmed of excess fat
1   teaspoon minced fresh dill
    Salt to taste
    Pepper to taste
1   cup water

PLACE ONIONS IN A DUTCH OVEN. Lay brisket on top. Sprinkle with dill, salt, and pepper. Add water. Cover and place over medium-high heat. Bring to a simmer. Lower heat and gently simmer for about 2½ hours or until meat is very tender and a rich, thick onion gravy has formed. Add water, ¼ cup at a time, if necessary, as brisket cooks.

Remove from heat. Slice brisket on the bias into thin slices and serve covered with onion gravy.

ROAST LEG OF LAMB WITH SPRING VEGETABLES

Serves 6 to 8.

1	6- to 8-pound leg of lamb
8	small cloves garlic, peeled (optional)
	Coarse salt to taste
	Cracked black pepper to taste
1	tablespoon celery seed

■ *Preheat oven to 500°F.*

WIPE LEG OF LAMB WITH A DAMP cloth. If desired, cut several small slits in the skin and insert garlic cloves into them. Generously coat skin with coarse salt, pepper, and celery seed.

Lay leg on rack in roasting pan, fat side up. Place in preheated oven and roast for 30 minutes. Lower heat to 350°F and roast for about 1½ hours or until meat thermometer registers 140°F for rare (or for about 2 hours or until meat thermometer registers 160°F for medium).

Remove from oven and let stand 15 minutes before carving. If desired, gravy can be prepared following the directions for roast beef gravy on page 16.

TO CARVE LEG OF LAMB

SLICE DOWN TO BONE AT THE FRONT and middle joints. Then, using a carving knife, make a careful cut from joint to joint against the bone. Carve individual slices by cutting down to the bone against the grain.

SPRING VEGETABLES

Serves 6 to 8.

2	pounds tiny new potatoes
1	pound tiny turnips
1	pound baby carrots
1½	pounds tender young asparagus
½	cup unsalted butter
1	tablespoon fresh lemon juice
1	tablespoon minced fresh dill
	Salt to taste
	White pepper to taste

SCRUB POTATOES, TURNIPS, AND CAR-rots. Trim stem ends from turnips and carrots. Wash asparagus. Trim stalks by breaking off tough ends and carefully peeling off the skin around the ends to make a neat stem.

Place potatoes, turnips, and carrots in rapidly boiling salted water to cover. Cover, lower heat, and simmer for about 10 minutes or until vegetables are just tender. Drain well and keep warm.

Place asparagus in a steamer basket over boiling water. Cover and cook for about 4 minutes or

just until tips are tender. Remove from heat and let stand another 5 minutes or until stalks are just tender. Keep warm.

Melt butter in a small saucepan over low heat. When melted, add lemon juice, dill, salt, and white pepper. Stir to blend and keep warm.

Place vegetables on a serving platter in a uniform pattern. Drizzle with melted dill butter and serve with roast leg of lamb.

Roast Leg of Lamb with Spring Vegetables. Delicious served with gravy.

TWO KINDS OF HAM

■

Serves 4 to 6.

1   10- to 12-pound country ham, *or*
1   10-pound commercially prepared precooked ham
    Approximately ¼ cup whole cloves
1   cup Madeira
1   cup brown sugar, tightly packed
2   teaspoons dry mustard
1   teaspoon ground cinnamon
½   teaspoon ground ginger
1½ cups dried bread crumbs
2   cups apple cider

FOR COUNTRY HAM: PURVEYORS OF traditional Smithfield, Virginia, or country hams will have their own instructions for preparation on the sack that encloses the ham. However, all country hams must be soaked at least 12 hours in cold water and then placed in boiling water to cover for at least an additional 20 minutes per pound. Allow ham to cool in cooking liquid, then remove. Cut away excess rind and fat from cooled ham and proceed with baking instructions. If the specific prebaking instructions for the ham you purchased are different from these, please follow those.

■ *Preheat oven to 375°F.*

Use a sharp knife to score top of ham in a crosshatched pattern. Place a whole clove in the center of each section. Place ham on rack in roasting pan. Combine Madeira, brown sugar, dry mustard, cinnamon, and ginger. When well combined, generously coat top of ham. Sprinkle with bread crumbs. Pour apple cider into the roasting pan. Place in preheated oven and roast for about 45 minutes or until meat is heated through and top is golden.

TO CARVE HAM

MAKE DEEP CUTS AT EACH END TO the bone, then run the carving knife along the bone from end to end. Carve slices by cutting down to the bone against the grain. Serve ham hot or cold.

ROAST LOIN OF VEAL

■

Serves 4 to 6.

1   6-pound loin of veal
¼   cup fresh sage leaves
    Cracked black pepper to taste
4   strips lean bacon
2   cups white wine

■ *Preheat oven to 450°F.*

WIPE VEAL WITH DAMP CLOTH. USE A knife to make several slits in the meat. Push fresh sage leaves into the slits. Season veal with pepper. Lay remaining sage leaves on top and cover with bacon.

Place on rack in roasting pan. Pour wine into pan and place in preheated oven for 15 minutes. Lower heat to 350°F and roast for about 2 hours or until meat thermometer registers 175°F. Remove from oven and let rest for 10 minutes. Remove bacon and discard. Slice and serve immediately.

NOTE: If desired, gravy can be prepared following instructions for roast beef gravy on page 16.

MIXED GRILL

A MIXED GRILL TRADITIONALLY HAS lamb, kidneys, and bacon as starring components. However, you can use any combination of meats with mushrooms, onions, and/or cherry tomatoes. For this you will need two metal skewers per person.

2   well-trimmed baby lamb chops
    per person
1   veal kidney, halved, per person
2   chicken livers per person
1   1½-inch-thick piece of fillet of beef,
    halved, per person
4   large mushroom caps per person
2   pearl onions, peeled, per person
1   cup olive oil
1   tablespoon minced garlic
¼   cup minced onion
2   bay leaves
1   teaspoon chopped fresh rosemary
1   tablespoon fresh lemon juice
    Salt to taste
    Pepper to taste
    Maître d'Hôtel Butter*

PLACE MEAT, MUSHROOM CAPS, AND pearl onions in a nonreactive bowl. Add olive oil, garlic, onion, bay leaves, rosemary, lemon juice, and salt and pepper. Toss to coat. Cover and let stand for 1 hour.

Thread each skewer with a lamb chop, mushroom cap, kidney piece, pearl onion, chicken liver, mushroom cap, and fillet slice.

For grilling: Preheat grill. When all skewers are complete, place on hot grill and cook, turning frequently, for about 6 minutes or until meat is crusty and just cooked through. Serve hot with a pat of Maître d'Hôtel Butter on each skewer.

For indoor cooking: Preheat broiler. Place skewers on broiler pan about 3 inches from flame. Broil, turning frequently, for about 6 minutes or until meat is crusty and just cooked through. Serve hot with a pat of Maître d'Hôtel Butter on each skewer.

MAÎTRE D'HÔTEL BUTTER

Makes approximately ½ cup.

½   cup softened unsalted butter
1½ tablespoons fresh lemon juice
2   tablespoons minced fresh parsley
    Salt to taste
    White pepper to taste

MIX BUTTER WITH LEMON JUICE. Blend in remaining ingredients until well combined. Cover and refrigerate until just firm. Roll into a log and cut into slices. Cover and freeze until ready to use.

LONDON BROIL

▬

Serves 4 to 6.

1   2½- to 3-pound, 1½-inch-thick
    rump steak or well-trimmed flank
    steak
    Salt to taste
    Cracked black pepper to taste
    Sautéed Mushrooms*

■ *Preheat broiler.*

GENEROUSLY COAT STEAK WITH SALT
and pepper. Place steak on broiler
pan about 3 inches from flame.
Broil rump steak for about 8 to 10
minutes per side for medium. (Rump
steak is generally tenderer if cooked
to at least medium.) Flank steak
should require no more than 5 minutes per side for rare. Turn steaks
only once. Remove from heat. Let
rest for 3 minutes. Slice very thin
on the diagonal, against the grain.

   Place on warm serving platter
and coat with Sautéed Mushrooms.

   NOTE: You may want to use a
commercial meat tenderizer on
rump steak as it sometimes can be a
bit tough.

**The Perfect Steak dressed with
parsley and cherry tomatoes.**

SAUTÉED MUSHROOMS

▬

Makes about 2 cups.

1   tablespoon butter
1   tablespoon olive oil
2   tablespoons minced shallots
1   tablespoon minced fresh parsley
3   cups sliced fresh mushrooms (either
    commercial white mushrooms or
    wild mushrooms of any kind, or a
    mixture of both)
    Salt to taste
    Pepper to taste
1   teaspoon fresh lemon juice

HEAT BUTTER AND OLIVE OIL IN HEAVY
sauté pan over medium heat. When
hot, add shallots and parsley. Sauté
for 3 minutes. Add mushrooms,
salt, and pepper. Cover and let cook
for about 10 minutes or until mushrooms are soft and liquid has begun
to flow. Uncover and cook, stirring
frequently, for 5 more minutes or
until liquid has almost evaporated.
Stir in lemon juice. Remove from
heat and serve immediately.

THE PERFECT STEAK

▬

Serves 4.

4   8-ounce, 1-inch-thick sirloin steaks
3   tablespoons canola oil
    Salt to taste
    Pepper to taste

■ *Preheat broiler or grill.*

TRIM STEAKS OF FAT AND SILVER SKIN.
Rub with oil and season with salt,
and pepper.

   Place steaks on broiler rack 3½
inches from flame. Broil, turning
once, for 4 minutes per side for rare,
6 minutes for medium, and 9 minutes for well done. Serve immediately.

   For grilling: Preheat grill. Place
steaks on hot grill and cook, turning
once, for about 6 minutes or until
meat is crusty and just cooked
through.

   NOTE: If you do not have a
broiler or a grill, purchase a ridged
cast-iron pan made specifically to
"broil" on top of the stove. Heat the
pan over high heat until red hot.
Add steaks and cook for the same
amount of time as above, pouring
off grease as it forms to keep steak
from frying in its own fat instead of
broiling.

The Perfect Hamburger and its Variations

Serves 6.

2   pounds very lean ground sirloin
⅓   cup ice water
    Coarse salt to taste
    Cracked pepper to taste

■ *Preheat broiler.*

COMBINE ALL INGREDIENTS. FORM into six firm patties. Place hamburgers on broiler rack and broil for about 3 minutes per side for rare, 4 minutes per side for medium, and 5 minutes per side for well done. Serve immediately.

If you choose to cook hamburgers on top of your stove, do so as directed for sirloin steak, on page 23

NOTE: I allow ⅓ pound meat per person. You can, if desired, cut allowance to ¼ pound per person.

VARIATIONS:
1. Add ½ cup minced red onion and/or 2 tablespoons minced fresh parsley.
2. Add ½ cup minced onion, 2 tablespoons minced fresh cilantro, and 1 minced jalapeño or serrano pepper.
3. Add ½ cup catsup, 1 tablespoon Worcestershire sauce, 1 tablespoon Dijon mustard, 1 tablespoon grated onion, 2 tablespoons dark beer, and ¾ cup dried bread crumbs.
4. Form patties around a 1-inch square piece of cheese (cheddar, jack, or brie).
5. Thirty seconds before burgers are done, place one slice of cheese of choice on top and allow it to melt.

MEAT LOAF AND ITS VARIATIONS

Serves 4 to 6.

1½ pounds lean ground beef
½   pound ground veal
½   cup minced onion
½   cup chopped canned plum
    tomatoes
1   teaspoon minced fresh parsley
1   cup fine bread crumbs
1   large egg
¼   cup milk
    Salt to taste
    Pepper to taste

■ *Preheat oven to 375°F.*

COMBINE ALL INGREDIENTS UNTIL well blended. Form into a firm oval shape about 4-inches by 8-inches. Place in a baking dish with sides. Place in preheated oven and bake for about 1 hour or until top is nicely browned and meat has cooked through. Remove from oven and slice. Serve hot or cold.

VARIATIONS:
1. You may use all beef, all veal, all pork, or a combination of these meats.
2. Ground turkey or chicken may be used. If so, add 2 tablespoons melted butter or vegetable oil to moisten.
3. Cover loaf with three strips of raw bacon before baking.
4. When forming loaf, place three hard-boiled eggs in the middle.
5. Eliminate tomatoes and add 1 teaspoon grated lemon rind and ¼ teaspoon grated fresh nutmeg.
6. To make meat loaf gravy you may add either 1½ cups chopped canned plum tomatoes, ½ cup beef stock, and ¼ cup minced onions, or 1½ cups beef stock, 1 tablespoon tomato paste, ½ cup chopped fresh mushrooms, and 1 tablespoon minced onion to the pan before baking. If liquid evaporates too quickly, add more water or stock to make a thick gravy as the meat loaf cooks.

My Famous Fried Chicken

▬

Serves 4 to 6.

My Famous Fried Chicken isn't fried at all, it just seems to be. I've never had a complaint. In fact, everyone wants to know why my chicken is always so crisp, greaseless, and tender.

2   2½-pound frying chickens, cut up
     (or you may use breasts, legs,
     and/or thighs)
2   cups milk
¼   cup unflavored yogurt
2   large eggs
2   cups all-purpose flour
½   cup very fine cornmeal
1   tablespoon grated lemon rind
1   teaspoon ground tarragon
1   teaspoon paprika
     Coarse salt to taste
     Cracked black pepper to taste
1   cup unsalted butter or margarine
1   cup corn oil

Wash and dry chicken. Combine milk, yogurt, and eggs until well blended. Pour over chicken and allow to sit for 30 minutes.

Place flour, cornmeal, lemon rind, tarragon, paprika, and salt and pepper in large brown paper bag or in a bowl. Drop chicken pieces into the bag, a few at a time, and shake to coat. When well coated, place pieces on a platter. Do not crowd. When all pieces are coated, cover lightly and refrigerate for at least 2 hours.

■ *Preheat oven to 500°F.*

Cover cooling racks with paper towels and set aside.

Place ½ cup butter and ½ cup corn oil in each of two 10-inch by 15-inch baking pans with sides. Place in preheated oven and allow butter to melt. When melted, completely stir to combine. Add chicken pieces to hot butter and oil, without crowding. Allow to cook for about 20 minutes or until one side is golden. Turn and cook for another 15 minutes or until chicken is golden and crisp. Remove from oven and immediately place pieces on paper towel-covered racks to drain. Serve hot or at room temperature.

If you cannot fry all the chicken in the two pans, use fresh butter and corn oil to fry remaining pieces.

To make gravy: Drain off 3 tablespoons fat from baking pans. Discard remaining fat but reserve all crispy brown bits from pans. Place fat and brown bits in heavy frying pan over medium heat. Stir in 3 tablespoons all-purpose flour and cook, stirring constantly, for about 1 minute or until flour absorbs fat and begins to turn golden. Whisk in 2 cups warm milk. Cook, stirring constantly, for 5 minutes or until gravy is thick and flour is well blended. Serve hot.

NOTE: To make Maryland Fried Chicken, bake as directed. When chicken is done, drain off all fat except that required to make gravy. Place all chicken in a deep ovenproof pan. Make gravy as directed and pour over chicken. Cover and return to oven for 10 minutes. Serve hot.

AUNTIE'S FRIED CHICKEN

▬

Serves 4 to 6.

MY HUSBAND'S EIGHTY-FIVE-YEAR-OLD aunt, Annie, makes truly wonderful real Southern fried chicken. Her recipe is foolproof: A mess of chicken, lots of all-purpose flour, lots of salt, lots of pepper, lots of hot grease. Which translates to:

2	2½-pound frying chickens, cut up
2	cups all-purpose flour
1½	tablespoons salt (or to taste)
1	tablespoon pepper (or to taste)
	Approximately 4½ cups solid vegetable shortening

WASH AND DRY CHICKEN. COMBINE flour, salt, and pepper. Roll chicken in seasoned flour. Melt 1½ cups solid shortening in each of three frying pans over medium-high heat. When sizzling hot, add chicken. Do not crowd pans. Cover and let cook for about 20 minutes. Turn and cook for another 20 minutes or until chicken is golden. Remove from pans and drain on paper towels.

BARBECUED SPARERIBS

■

Serves 6.

THERE IS ALMOST NOTHING AS TASTY as great open-pit barbecued ribs. However, since we generally have to content ourselves with summer's backyard gas grill and winter's kitchen oven, I developed this method that comes close to those fabulous, meaty, falling-off-the-bones ribs.

6   pounds lean meaty pork spareribs (or baby back or beef ribs)
     Salt to taste
     Pepper to taste
¼   cup apple cider vinegar
¼   cup brown sugar
     Barbecue Sauce*

■ *Preheat oven to 350°F.*

CUT RACKS INTO INDIVIDUAL RIBS. Toss with salt, pepper, vinegar, and brown sugar. Tightly seal in heavy-duty aluminum foil and place on a rack in a roasting pan with 1 inch of water. Place in preheated oven and bake for 1½ hours, replacing water as necessary to keep at least ½ inch of water in at all times.

Remove from oven and unwrap. Remove the rack and pour off any water. Return ribs to pan. Pour on Barbecue Sauce and toss to coat. Cover pan and return to oven. Lower heat to 300°F and bake for about 30 minutes. Uncover and bake for another 15 minutes or until meat is falling off the bones and a bit crisp on the edge. Remove from oven and serve immediately.

BARBECUE SAUCE

■

Makes approximately 6 cups.

2   tablespoons butter
1   cup minced onion
3   cups catsup
1   cup beer
¾   cup light brown sugar
¾   cup cider vinegar
3   tablespoons Worcestershire sauce
1   tablespoon maple syrup
1½   tablespoons chili powder
2   teaspoons dry mustard
      Salt to taste
      Pepper to taste
      Tabasco™¹ sauce to taste

MELT BUTTER IN A HEAVY SAUCEPAN over medium heat. When melted, add onion. Cook, stirring frequently, for 5 minutes or until onion is very soft. Stir in remaining ingredients. Bring to a boil. When boiling, lower heat and cook for about 45 minutes or until sauce is thick and flavors are blended.

NOTE: You may replace syrup with honey, beer with water, and salt with soy sauce, if desired. Barbecue Sauce may be made in advance of use, then covered and refrigerated for up to one week.

Meaty Barbecued Spareribs garnished with parsley and served with buttered corn-on-the-cob and Barbecue Sauce.

Stuffed Cabbage or Peppers

Perfect Pot Roast

Old-fashioned Beef Stew

Tamale Pie

Chili Con Carne

Goulash

Shepherd's Pie

Corned Beef and Cabbage

New England Boiled Dinner

Potted Veal

Chicken Fricassee with
Dumplings

Oyster Stew

Irish Stew

Chicken Gumbo

ONE-DISH MEALS

STUFFED CABBAGE OR PEPPERS

■■■■

Serves 6.

12 large green cabbage leaves (or 6 large green bell peppers)
1   pound lean ground beef
1   cup cooked rice
1½ cups minced onion
2   tablespoons minced fresh parsley
1   large egg
1   tablespoon tomato paste
    Salt to taste
    Pepper to taste
3   cups canned plum tomatoes with juice
1   cup beef stock
2   tablespoons light brown sugar
1   tablespoon wine vinegar

PLACE CABBAGE LEAVES IN RAPIDLY boiling water for 1 minute to just soften. Drain and pat dry. (Or, wash peppers. Cut off stem end and remove seeds and white membrane. Rinse peppers and wipe dry.)

Combine ground beef, rice, ½ cup minced onion, parsley, egg, tomato paste, and salt and pepper. When well combined, place a portion of meat mixture into each cabbage leaf. Fold over, then fold in sides and roll. Close with a wooden toothpick. (Or fill peppers to the top of cut end, mounding slightly.)

■ *Preheat oven to 350°F.*

Combine remaining onions, tomatoes, beef stock, brown sugar, vinegar, and salt and pepper in a Dutch oven. Place peppers, stuffed top up, in tomato mixture. Place uncovered in preheated oven and bake for 45 minutes or until meat stuffing is cooked. Follow the same instructions for cabbage except bake covered. Serve hot.

Stuffed peppers (or cabbage) may be made in advance of use. Store either covered and refrigerated for up to two days or tightly sealed and frozen for up to three months.

NOTE: Ground beef may be replaced with ground veal, pork, lamb, chicken, or turkey. If so, replace beef stock with appropriate substitution. The meat stuffing may be used to fill squash, either summer or winter, and eggplant. For winter squash, the baking time should be increased to about 1½ hours.

Stuffed Cabbage in tomato sauce, sprinkled with minced parsley.

Perfect Pot Roast

▬

Serves 6 to 8.

2   tablespoons vegetable oil
1   6-pound beef rump roast
1   cup beef broth
2   cups water
1   large yellow onion, peeled and
    chopped
2   large carrots, cleaned and
    chopped
2   tablespoons tomato paste
¼   teaspoon ground marjoram (or 2
    sprigs fresh)
¼   teaspoon ground thyme (or 2 sprigs
    fresh)
1   bay leaf
    Pinch ground cinnamon
    Salt to taste
    Pepper to taste
18 to 24 pearl onions, peeled
18 baby carrots, peeled
12 tiny new potatoes
1   tablespoon cornstarch dissolved in
    1 tablespoon water *or*
    1 tablespoon butter kneaded into
    1 tablespoon all-purpose flour, if
    necessary

Heat oil in a heavy Dutch oven over medium heat. When hot, add meat. Lower heat and cook, turning frequently, until all sides are lightly browned. Remove meat from pan and drain off all fat. Carefully wipe pan clean with a paper towel.

Return roast to Dutch oven and add beef broth, water, yellow onion, carrots, tomato paste, herbs, bay leaf, salt, and pepper, and stir to blend. Cover and place Dutch oven over medium heat on top of stove or in a preheated 350°F oven. Cook at a low simmer for about 2 hours or until meat is almost tender.

Remove meat from Dutch oven and skim off excess fat. Strain liquids through a fine sieve, pressing out as much broth as possible. Discard solids. Return roast and strained liquid to Dutch oven. Add pearl onions, baby carrots, and new potatoes. Place over medium-high heat and bring to a boil. Cover and lower heat. Simmer for about 15 minutes or until vegetables are tender.

Remove meat and vegetables from liquid and keep warm. If liquid is not as thick as you would like, whisk in dissolved cornstarch or softened butter kneaded into flour, a small amount at a time, until gravy is as thick as you desire.

Slice meat and arrange down the center of a warm serving platter. Place vegetables around the edge and lightly coat with gravy. Pass remaining gravy on the side.

NOTE: Red wine or a hearty beer may replace one-half of the cooking liquid. Celery, fresh peas, and/or turnips may also be added with other vegetables.

OLD-FASHIONED BEEF STEW

—— *Serves 6.*

2 pounds boneless, lean beef stew meat, cut into 1½-inch cubes
1 cup diced onions
¼ cup flour
  Salt to taste
  Pepper to taste
2 tablespoons vegetable oil
1 pound carrots, peeled and cubed
1 pound potatoes, peeled and cubed
1 10-ounce package frozen petite peas, thawed

COMBINE MEAT, ONIONS, FLOUR, SALT, and pepper, and toss until meat and onions are well coated.

Heat oil in a heavy saucepan with lid. When hot, add beef and onions, a few pieces at a time. Fry, stirring frequently, for about 4 minutes or until meat has browned. Drain on paper towels.

When all meat and onions have been browned, carefully wipe excess fat from pan. Return meat and onions to pan and place over medium-high heat. Add water to just cover and bring to a boil. When boiling, lower heat and simmer for about 30 minutes or until meat just begins to tenderize. Add carrots and potatoes and cook for 20 more minutes or until meat and vegetables are quite tender. Stir in peas and cook for another minute or until peas are just heated through. If the broth is not thick enough, work 1 tablespoon softened butter into 1 tablespoon all-purpose flour and stir into stew, a small amount at a time, until gravy is as thick as you desire. Serve hot.

NOTE: Beef stew may be made in advance of use. Store, either covered and refrigerated for up to two days, or tightly sealed and frozen for up to three months.

VARIATIONS:
1. Beer, red wine, or beef stock may replace the water. Or beer, wine, and beef stock each may be used in combination with water and/or stock.
2. Whole pearl onions may be added with carrots and potatoes.
3. Any other combination of vegetables may be substituted or used in conjunction with carrots, potatoes, or peas.
4. Potatoes may be replaced with dumplings (see page 42) or dumplings may be served in addition.
5. One cup tomato puree may be added with the water.
6. One teaspoon minced garlic, 1 tablespoon minced fresh parsley, 1 bay leaf, and ¼ teaspoon dried thyme may be added with the water.
7. Mushrooms may be used in addition to other vegetables, or 2 pounds of mushrooms can replace all vegetables except onions.

TAMALE PIE

◾

Serves 6.

1½	pounds lean ground beef
1	cup diced red onion
½	cup diced green bell pepper
1	tablespoon minced garlic
1	cup cooked corn kernels
1	tablespoon chili powder
1	teaspoon ground cumin
	Pinch oregano
	Crushed red pepper flakes to taste
2	cups tomato puree
½	cup pitted black olives
¼	cup chopped canned green chilies
	Salt to taste
	Pepper to taste
¾	cup cornmeal
2	cups cold water
1	cup shredded sharp cheddar or Monterey jack cheese
1	tablespoon butter

PLACE GROUND MEAT IN A HEAVY sauté pan over medium-high heat. Cook, stirring frequently, for about 5 minutes or until meat begins to brown. Add onion, green pepper, and garlic and cook, stirring frequently, for another 10 minutes or until vegetables are quite soft. Stir in corn, chili powder, cumin, oregano, and red pepper flakes. When well combined, stir in tomato puree, olives, green chilies, and salt and pepper. Cover and cook, stirring occasionally, for about 30 minutes or until quite thick and flavors have blended. Pour into a 9-inch-square baking pan and set aside.

◾ *Preheat oven to 375°F.*

Stir cornmeal into cold water in a medium-sized saucepan. Place over high heat and bring to a boil. When boiling, lower heat to a simmer and cook for about 5 minutes or until quite thick. Whisk in cheese and butter. Immediately spoon over meat. Place in preheated oven and bake for 30 minutes or until golden. Serve hot.

Spicy Tamale Pie, perfect topped with melted sharp cheddar cheese.

CHILI CON CARNE

Serves 6 to 8.

1 pound dried pinto beans
2 pounds coarsely ground beef
1½ cups chopped onions
1 tablespoon minced garlic
1 jalapeño pepper, stemmed,
   seeded, and chopped (or to taste)
¼ cup chili powder
2 teaspoons ground cumin
   Pinch oregano
   Tabasco™ sauce to taste
   Salt to taste
   Pepper to taste
5 cups canned tomatoes with juice

RINSE BEANS. COVER WITH COLD water and soak for at least 4 hours, changing water twice. Place in a large saucepan. Cover with cold water and place over high heat. Bring to a boil. When boiling, lower heat to a simmer. Cover and cook for about 1 hour or until beans are tender.

Place ground beef in a heavy sauté pan over high heat. Cook, stirring frequently, for about 10 minutes or until beef has begun to brown. Add onions, garlic, and jalapeño pepper and cook for an-

other 3 minutes. Add chili powder, cumin, oregano, Tabasco™, and salt and pepper, and stir to combine. Scrape into beans. Add tomatoes and return to medium heat. Bring to a simmer and cook for about 1 hour or until flavors have blended and chili is quite thick. Serve hot.

NOTE: Chili is best made in advance of use. Store either covered and refrigerated for up to four days or tightly sealed and frozen for up to three months.

GOULASH

Serves 6.

GOULASH HAS NOW BECOME A GE-neric term for a mixture combining meat, onions, sour cream, and pa-prika. Hungarian goulash contains beef, but no flour or sour cream. Viennese goulash has veal, flour, and sour cream. My Mom used the word goulash for any combination of leftovers. It sounded much more appetizing than "leftovers, again."

2 pounds lean veal stew meat, cut
   into 2-inch cubes
½ cup all-purpose flour
   Salt to taste
   Pepper to taste
1 tablespoon fine Hungarian paprika
2 tablespoons vegetable oil
3 cups diced onions
1 cup water
1 cup chopped, skinless, seedless
   tomatoes
1½ cups sour cream
1 teaspoon minced fresh parsley

COMBINE VEAL, FLOUR, SALT AND pepper, and paprika. Toss to coat.

Heat oil in a heavy Dutch oven over medium-high heat. When hot, brown veal, a few pieces at a time, for about 4 minutes or until well browned on all sides. Drain on pa-per towels.

When all veal is browned, add onions to pan and cook for 2 min-utes. Add water. Raise heat and bring to a boil, scraping brown bits from the bottom of the pan as you go. When boiling, add veal and tomatoes. Lower heat and simmer for 1 hour or until veal is very ten-der. Remove from heat. Stir in sour cream and parsley and serve imme-diately with buttered noodles, if desired.

SHEPHERD'S PIE

Serves 6.

4	cups cooked ground beef (or any cooked ground meat)
1	cup grated cooked potatoes
1	cup grated cooked carrots
¼	cup grated raw onion
1	tablespoon minced fresh parsley
1½	cups beef stock and 1 tablespoon cornstarch
	Salt to taste
	Pepper to taste
2	cups mashed potatoes (page 72)
2	tablespoons melted butter
2	tablespoons bread crumbs

■ *Preheat oven to 350°F.*

GREASE A DEEP-DISH PIE PLATE AND set aside.

Combine meat, grated potatoes, carrots, onion, and parsley. Dissolve cornstarch in beef stock in a small saucepan over medium heat. Cook for about 3 minutes or until slightly thick. (Eliminate this step if using beef gravy.) Pour into meat mixture and stir to combine. Add salt and pepper.

Place in prepared pie plate and cover with mashed potatoes. Brush with melted butter and sprinkle with bread crumbs. Place in preheated oven and bake for about 20 minutes or until potatoes are golden and pie is heated through. Serve immediately.

CORNED BEEF AND CABBAGE

Serves 6.

1	3- to 4-pound corned beef brisket
1	large onion, peeled and stuck with 6 whole cloves
3	bay leaves
1	teaspoon peppercorns
½	cup maple syrup
1	large head cabbage, cored and cut into wedges
½	cup drained, prepared horseradish

RINSE CORNED BEEF AND TRIM OFF excess fat. Place in a Dutch oven with cold water to cover. Bring to a boil over high heat. When boiling, remove from heat and drain. Keep beef in Dutch oven. Cover with cold water. Add onion, bay leaves, and peppercorns. Bring to a boil over high heat. When boiling, reduce heat to a simmer. Cover and simmer for about 2 hours or until meat is very tender. Remove meat from broth and set aside. Strain off cooking broth and reserve 2 cups.

■ *Preheat oven to 375°F.*

Place corned beef on rack in a roasting pan. Brush with maple syrup and bake in preheated oven for about 20 minutes or until glazed. Remove from oven and keep warm.

Place reserved cooking broth in Dutch oven. Add cabbage and bring to a boil over high heat. When boiling, reduce heat and cook for about 5 minutes or until cabbage is tender and has absorbed the corned beef flavor. Drain cabbage, reserving broth.

Slice corned beef. Place down the center of a warm serving platter and surround with cabbage. Serve with horseradish and use the reserved broth as gravy.

New England Boiled Dinner

Serves 6.

1   3- to 4-pound corned beef brisket
¼   pound salt pork, diced
1   tablespoon black peppercorns
6   small carrots, peeled (or 3 large
    carrots, peeled and cubed)
3   turnips, peeled and quartered
6   small onions, peeled
6   small potatoes, peeled (or 3 large
    potatoes, quartered)
1   small green cabbage, cored and
    cut into wedges

RINSE AND DRY CORNED BEEF. TRIM off excess fat. Place in a Dutch oven with cold water to cover over high heat. Add salt pork and peppercorns. Cover and bring to a boil. When boiling, lower heat and gently simmer for 2½ hours. Add carrots, turnips, onions, and potatoes and cook for about 20 minutes or until vegetables are almost tender. Add

cabbage and cook for an additional 10 minutes or until cabbage is just tender.

When vegetables and cabbage are cooked, remove from heat. Remove meat from pan and carve into thin slices. Place down the center of a heated serving platter. Surround with vegetables and serve.

Potted Veal

Serves 6.

1   3-pound, 1-inch-thick veal steak
½   cup all-purpose flour
½   teaspoon paprika
¼   teaspoon dry mustard
    Salt to taste
    Pepper to taste
2   tablespoons canola oil
12 tiny onions
2   cups diced carrots
1   cup diced celery
1   cup sliced mushrooms
    Approximately 3 cups half-and-half
    or milk
½   cup sour cream

TRIM EXCESS FAT FROM VEAL STEAK. Combine flour, paprika, dry mustard, and salt and pepper. Dredge veal with seasoned flour. Lightly pound flour into meat with a mallet or the edge of a heavy plate.

Heat oil in a heavy, deep sauté pan over medium-high heat. When hot, brown veal steak for about 3 minutes per side or until well seared.

Remove meat and carefully wipe excess fat from pan. Return meat to pan. Cover with vegetables and half-and-half. Place over medium heat and bring to a simmer. Cover and simmer for about 45 minutes or until meat is very tender. Remove from heat and stir in sour cream. Serve immediately with buttered noodles, if desired.

New England Boiled Dinner.

CHICKEN FRICASSEE WITH DUMPLINGS

▬

Serves 6.

A TOUGH OLD BIRD OR STEWING HEN traditionally used for fricassee is now almost impossible to find. If you are able to obtain one from a local farm, cooking time should be increased by about 45 minutes. Dumplings may be substituted with noodles or rice.

6	pounds chicken pieces (breasts, thighs, and legs)
½	cup diced onion
2	stalks celery, sliced
1	carrot, diced
3	tablespoons minced fresh parsley
2	cups chicken stock
	Salt to taste
	Pepper to taste
2	cups all-purpose flour
1	tablespoon baking powder
¼	cup solid vegetable shortening
1	large egg
	Approximately 1 cup milk
1	tablespoon cornstarch dissolved in 1 tablespoon cold water (optional)

WASH AND DRY CHICKEN PIECES. Place in a Dutch oven with onion, celery, carrot, parsley, chicken stock, salt and pepper, and enough water to cover. Place over medium-high heat and bring to a boil. When boiling, cover and lower heat. Simmer for about 45 minutes or until chicken is very tender. Remove from heat.

Strain liquid back into pan and discard vegetables. Remove skin and bone from chicken, keeping meat in pieces that are as large as possible. Keep chicken warm.

Combine flour, baking powder, and salt to taste. Cut in shortening to make a crumbly dough. Stir in egg and enough milk to make a soft dough.

Return broth to high heat. When boiling, drop dumpling dough into bubbling broth by the tablespoonful (use a wet tablespoon to keep dough from sticking). When all the dough is in the broth, lower heat and cover. Simmer for 15 minutes. Do not remove cover. Remove from heat and uncover.

Place chicken meat on a warm serving platter. Surround with dumplings. If the broth is not thick enough to serve as gravy, stir in dissolved cornstarch and whisk over medium-high heat until thick. Generously cover chicken and dumplings with gravy and pass remaining gravy separately.

OYSTER STEW

━━

Serves 6.

1   quart shucked oysters with liquor
¾   cup unsalted butter
1   tablespoon minced celery
2   teaspoons Worcestershire sauce
½   teaspoon Tabasco™ sauce (or to
    taste)
½   teaspoon paprika
4   cups hot cream or half-and-half
    Salt to taste
    Pepper to taste

DRAIN OYSTERS, RESERVING LIQUOR.
Melt ½ cup unsalted butter in a
large, heavy saucepan over medium-
low heat. When melted, stir in celery, Worcestershire sauce, Tabasco™
sauce, and paprika and cook for
about 2 minutes. Add oysters and
cook for 3 minutes. Stir in oyster
liquor and cook for an additional 3
minutes or until oysters begin to
curl at the edges. Add hot cream
and cook for 1 minute. Stir in salt
and pepper with remaining butter.
Serve immediately.

IRISH STEW

━━

Serves 6.

TRADITIONALLY, IRISH STEW IS MADE
from the neck or shoulder lamb on
the bone. Although the bones do
make a tastier stew, I prefer boneless, lean lamb stew meat.

2½ pounds lean lamb stew meat, cut
    into 1½-inch cubes
2   pounds potatoes, peeled and cut
    into ¼-inch-thick slices
1   pound pearl onions, peeled (or 1
    pound large onions, peeled and
    sliced)
¼   cup minced fresh parsley
½   teaspoon dried ground thyme
    Salt to taste
    Pepper to taste
2   cups water

PLACE ONE-HALF OF THE LAMB IN THE
bottom of a Dutch oven. Cover
with one-half of the potatoes and
one-half of the onions. Use remaining lamb, potatoes, and onions to
make another layer. Add parsley,
thyme, and salt and pepper. Pour
water to cover all ingredients. Cover
and place over medium heat and
bring to a boil. When boiling, lower
heat to a simmer and cook for 1
hour or until lamb is very tender.
Check stew from time to time to
see if liquid is evaporating. If so,
add no more than ¼ cup water at a
time as stew should be quite thick.
Serve hot.

NOTE: You may also add 1
pound of carrots, peeled and sliced.
Irish Stew may be made in advance
of use. Store either covered and
refrigerated for up to two days or
tightly sealed and frozen for up to
three months.

Chicken Gumbo

———

Serves 6.

For years chicken gumbo has been made outside of the Deep South without gumbo filé, a traditional Louisiana staple. Gumbo just meant okra was a component of the recipe. With the recent interest in Cajun and Creole cooking, filé powder is now relatively easy to obtain in either the spice section of specialty or gourmet shops or by mail order. Adding ham, shrimp, and crab makes a more typical, down-home gumbo.

5	pounds chicken pieces (breasts, legs, and thighs) or a cut-up whole chicken
3	tablespoons vegetable oil or bacon fat
1	cup chopped onion
½	cup diced green bell pepper
½	cup diced red bell pepper
½	cup diced celery
¼	cup chopped scallions
1	tablespoon minced garlic
½	cup minced fresh parsley
4	cups canned plum tomatoes with juice
1	tablespoon Worcestershire sauce
1	teaspoon ground black pepper (or to taste)
½	teaspoon red pepper flakes (or to taste)
	Salt to taste
3	cups thinly sliced fresh okra
2	teaspoons filé powder

Wash and dry chicken pieces.

Heat oil in a Dutch oven over medium-high heat. When hot, add onion, green and red bell peppers, celery, scallions, garlic, and ¼ cup parsley. Cook, stirring frequently for about 7 minutes or until vegetables just begin to brown. Add chicken and continue to cook, stirring frequently, for about 5 minutes or until chicken has begun to brown. Add tomatoes, Worcestershire sauce, black pepper, red pepper flakes, salt, and enough water to just cover. Bring to a simmer. Cover and simmer for 30 minutes. Add okra and simmer for an additional 20 minutes or until chicken is tender and okra has cooked. Stir in filé powder, a bit at a time, to thicken the gravy. Add filé carefully, as it will thicken the gravy very quickly. Stir in remaining parsley and serve immediately over white rice, if desired.

NOTE: You can also add 1 cup raw rice when you add okra. If so, do not add filé powder or gumbo will be too thick. Chicken Gumbo may be made in advance of use. Store either covered and refrigerated for up to two days or tightly sealed and frozen for up to three months.

Savory Chicken Gumbo, served on a bed of rice.

Pepper Steak

Lasagna

Meatballs and Spaghetti

Sloppy Joes

Hash

Chicken Croquettes

Swiss Steak

Franks and Beans

Swedish Meatballs

Creamed Chipped Beef
on Toast

Chicken a la King

Liver and Onions

Shrimp Wiggle

Macaroni and Cheese

Mom's Cheese Casserole

Cheese Souffle

3

MAIN DISH

FAVORITES

PEPPER STEAK

—

Serves 6.

PEPPER STEAK SEEMS TO BE EVERY American mother's cross-cultural answer to Chinese food.

1	1½-inch-thick lean top-round steak
3	tablespoons vegetable oil
¼	cup light soy sauce
½	cup beef stock
1	teaspoon minced garlic
2	large green bell peppers, stemmed, seeded, and sliced
1	large onion, peeled and sliced
½	cup sliced celery
3	whole ripe tomatoes, cored and quartered
½	cup chopped scallions
1	tablespoon cornstarch dissolved in 1 tablespoon cold water

SLICE STEAK INTO STRIPS ABOUT 3 inches long and ¼ inch thick.

Heat oil in a deep-sided sauté pan over medium-high heat. When hot, add beef strips. Sauté, turning frequently, for about 5 minutes until all sides of meat strips are brown. Drain meat on paper towels and carefully wipe excess fat from pan.

Return meat to pan. Add soy sauce, beef stock, and garlic. Place over medium-high heat and bring to a boil. When boiling, lower heat, cover, and simmer for about 30 minutes or until meat is tender. Stir in peppers, onion, and celery. Cover and cook for about 5 minutes or until vegetables are crisp-tender. Add tomatoes and scallions. Stir in dissolved cornstarch. Raise heat and bring to a boil, stirring frequently but being careful not to break up vegetables. Boil for no more than 1 minute to slightly thicken. Serve hot with boiled rice, if desired.

Colorful Pepper Steak, served over boiled white rice.

LASAGNA

━━━

Serves 8.

2	pounds mozzarella cheese
1	pound ricotta cheese – cottage cheese
2	cups grated Parmesan cheese
2	large eggs
½	cup minced fresh Italian parsley
	Pepper to taste
1	pound lasagna noodles
1	recipe Tomato Sauce*

CUT 1 POUND OF THE MOZZARELLA into cubes. Cut the remaining pound into slices and set aside.

Combine mozzarella cubes, ricotta, 1½ cups grated Parmesan, eggs, parsley, and pepper. Set aside.

■ *Preheat oven to 350°F.*

Cook lasagna noodles according to package directions for al dente. When cooked, drain and rinse under hot running water. Return to pan and cover with cold water.

Drain lasagna noodles, one strip at a time, on paper towels. When drained, lay enough strips lengthwise to cover bottom of pan. Cover with one-third of the combined cheeses and then with a layer of Tomato Sauce. Make two more layers of noodles, cheeses, and Tomato Sauce, ending with a final layer of noodles. Cover top with sliced mozzarella and remaining Parmesan cheese.

Place in preheated oven and bake for 40 minutes or until bubbly and cheese is lightly browned. (If cheese begins to brown too quickly, cover top with aluminum foil. Remove foil about 5 minutes before lasagna is ready to be removed from oven.)

Remove lasagna from oven and allow to sit for 15 minutes before cutting into serving pieces.

NOTE: You can make a vegetarian lasagna by replacing noodles with thinly sliced zucchini that has been blanched for 1 minute in boiling, salted water or with thin slices of eggplant that have been sautéed in olive oil for 2 minutes per side. Drain either vegetable well before making lasagna layers.

TOMATO SAUCE

━━━

Makes approximately 12 cups.

2	tablespoons olive oil
1	cup diced onion
4	cloves garlic, peeled and minced
½	cup grated carrots (optional)
¼	cup minced fresh Italian parsley
1	tablespoon dried basil (or 3 tablespoons minced fresh)
1	teaspoon dried ground oregano (or 1 sprig fresh)
2	1-pound-13-ounce cans Italian plum tomatoes
2	1-pound-13-ounce cans crushed tomatoes
¼	cup tomato paste
1	bay leaf
	Red pepper flakes to taste
1	tablespoon sugar
	Salt to taste
	Pepper to taste

thyme

Heat olive oil in large, heavy saucepan over medium-high heat. When hot, add onion and garlic and sauté for about 4 minutes or until soft. Stir in carrots, parsley, basil, and oregano and cook for 3 minutes. Add tomatoes, tomato paste, bay leaf, red pepper flakes, sugar, and salt and pepper.

Bring to a boil. When boiling, lower heat to a simmer and cook for about 1½ hours or until flavors are well blended. Discard bay leaf. Serve hot. Tomato Sauce may be made in advance of use. Store either covered and refrigerated for up to three days or tightly sealed and frozen for up to three months.

NOTE: This tomato sauce may be used as is, as a sauce for any cooked pasta. Pass grated Parmesan cheese on the side. If you wish to make meat sauce for spaghetti rather than meatballs, first sauté 2 pounds ground meat, then proceed with Tomato Sauce recipe. You may also add ½ pound sliced mushrooms to the basic recipe. Sauté mushrooms for 3 minutes after the onion and garlic and before adding carrots.

MEATBALLS AND SPAGHETTI

Serves 6.

1	pound lean ground pork or veal
1	pound lean ground beef
1	large onion, peeled and grated
½	cup grated carrot
¼	cup minced fresh Italian parsley
1	tablespoon minced garlic
1	cup fresh bread crumbs
1	large egg
1	teaspoon dried basil
¼	teaspoon dried ground oregano
	Salt to taste
	Pepper to taste
3	tablespoons olive oil
	Tomato Sauce*
1	pound dried spaghetti number nine, linguine, or perciatelli (or other heavy pasta)
1	cup grated Parmesan cheese (optional)

Combine meat, onion, carrot, parsley, garlic, bread crumbs, egg, basil, oregano, and salt and pepper. When well combined, shape into 1½- to 2-inch balls.

Heat olive oil in a heavy sauté pan over medium-high heat. When hot, add meatballs, a few at a time, and fry, turning frequently, for about 5 minutes or until well browned. Drain on paper towels.

Place hot Tomato Sauce in a deep saucepan over medium-high heat. When simmering, add meatballs. Bring to a boil. When boiling, lower heat to a simmer. Cover and simmer for about 30 minutes or until meatballs are cooked through.

Place spaghetti in 6 quarts of rapidly boiling salted water. Boil for about 9 minutes for al dente (firm but cooked). Drain and rinse under hot running water. Drain well.

Place spaghetti on a warm serving plate. Top with sauce and meatballs. Pass extra sauce and meatballs with grated Parmesan cheese, if desired.

NOTE: For low-cholesterol diets, meatballs may be made with ground poultry. Meatballs and sauce may be made in advance of use. Store either covered and refrigerated for up to two days or tightly sealed and frozen for up to three months.

SLOPPY JOES

———

Serves 6.

1½ pounds lean ground beef
1   cup minced onion
½   cup diced green bell pepper
1   clove garlic, peeled and minced
1   cup catsup
     Salt to taste
     Pepper to taste
6   crusty rolls, split and toasted

PLACE BEEF IN A HEAVY SAUTÉ PAN over medium-high heat. Cook, stirring frequently, for about 10 minutes or until meat begins to brown. Add onion, bell pepper, and garlic and cook for an additional 10 minutes. Stir in catsup and salt and pepper and continue to cook for about 3 minutes or until heated through. Serve open-faced on toasted rolls.

HASH

———

Serves 6.

HASH IS SIMPLY A TASTY LEFTOVER. IT is made with any type of leftover roast meat. Beef and corned beef are the best known, but lamb—my favorite—chicken, and turkey make great hash dinners. Every cook has his or her own method. This is mine.

2   tablespoons butter
¾   cup diced onion
3   cups cubed, roasted meat
3   cups cubed, boiled, or roasted
     potatoes
     Salt to taste
     Pepper to taste

MELT BUTTER IN A HEAVY SKILLET over medium-high heat. When melted, add onion. Fry, stirring frequently, for about 6 minutes or until onion begins to brown. Add meat and potatoes and cook, stirring frequently, for about 15 minutes or until crisp. Add salt and pepper and serve immediately.

VARIATIONS:
1. Combine all ingredients with ½ cup leftover gravy or cream. Melt butter as above and when melted, firmly pat meat mixture into skillet. Place over low heat and cook for about 30 minutes or until bottom is crusty. Flip over and serve as a large pancake.
2. Combine all ingredients as above, but place in a greased 2-quart casserole and bake in a preheated 350°F oven for 35 minutes or until crisp.
3. For Red Flannel Hash: Using corned beef, combine ingredients as above with the addition of 1½ cups chopped, cooked beets.
4. Any other leftover roasted vegetables such as carrots, celery, parsnips, or onion may be added.

Hearty Hash, made with chicken.

CHICKEN CROQUETTES

——

Serves 6.

4 cups finely chopped cooked chicken
2 teaspoons fresh lemon juice
1 tablespoon minced fresh parsley
1 tablespoon minced onion
  Tabasco™ sauce to taste
  Salt to taste
  Pepper to taste
½ cup unsalted butter
⅔ cup flour
1 cup warm cream or half-and-half
½ cup warm chicken stock
2 large eggs
  Approximately 2 cups fine bread crumbs
  Approximately 4 cups vegetable oil

COMBINE CHICKEN, LEMON JUICE, parsley, onion, Tabasco™ sauce, and salt and pepper and set aside.

Melt butter in a medium-sized saucepan over medium-high heat. When melted, stir in flour until well blended. Whisk in cream and chicken stock. Cook, whisking constantly, for 5 minutes or until sauce is very thick. Add chicken, a bit at a time, stirring to blend until you have a soft but malleable mixture. Cover and refrigerate for 1 hour or until well chilled.

When well chilled, form into balls, cone shapes, or logs using no more than ¼ cup mixture per portion. Place bread crumbs in a shallow bowl. Combine eggs with ¼ cup water. Dip each croquette into bread crumbs, then egg mixture, then again dip in bread crumbs. Place on a plate covered with wax paper and refrigerate for 30 minutes.

Heat oil in a deep-fat fryer over high heat to 365°F on a food thermometer. Fry croquettes, a few at a time, for about 1 minute or until golden-brown. Drain on paper towels and keep warm until all croquettes are cooked. Serve hot, as is, or with any zesty sauce or gravy you desire.

NOTE: You may make croquettes from any cooked meat or fish. Follow above recipe and method. Replace chicken stock with additional half-and-half or with the appropriate stock.

SWISS STEAK

━━━

Serves 6.

I STILL WONDER WHY THIS STEAK IS called Swiss. It has always seemed to me to be much more Mediterranean.

1   1½-inch-thick, 3-pound round
    steak
½   cup all-purpose flour
    Salt to taste
    Pepper to taste
1   tablespoon vegetable oil
2   large onions, peeled and sliced
1   clove garlic, peeled and minced
3   cups canned plum tomatoes with
    juice
1   cup beef stock

TRIM ANY EXCESS FAT FROM STEAK and cut into individual portions.

Combine flour and salt and pepper, and, using a mallet, pound the seasoned flour into both sides of the steak pieces.

Heat oil in a heavy, deep-sided sauté pan or Dutch oven with lid. When hot, add floured steak. Sear each side for about 3 minutes or until brown. Drain steak on paper towels and carefully wipe excess fat from pan. Do not scrape off any of the browned bits.

Return steak to pan and add remaining ingredients. Cover and place over medium-high heat. When tomatoes begin to simmer, lower heat and cook for about 1½ hours or until meat is tender when a fork is inserted into it. Taste and adjust seasonings. Serve immediately.

NOTE: You may also cook Swiss Steak in a preheated 350°F oven for about the same amount of time.

FRANKS AND BEANS

———

Serves 6.

THIS IS MUCH MORE THAN THE OPEN-a-can, open-a-package, single-cook's-easy-dinner.

1	pound dried navy beans
3	cups beer
1	cup catsup
1	cup minced onion
½	pound salt pork or rack bacon, cubed
½	cup light brown sugar
½	cup molasses
1½	teaspoons dry mustard
½	teaspoon Worcestershire sauce
	Salt to taste
	Pepper to taste
1	pound frankfurters (or bratwurst)

RINSE BEANS. COVER WITH COLD water and allow to soak for at least 4 hours or overnight, changing water twice. When soft, pour off soaking water and drain beans well.

Place beans with about 6 cups of cold water in a heavy saucepan over high heat. Bring to a boil. When boiling, lower heat and simmer for about 1 hour or until beans are tender. Remove from heat and drain, reserving liquid.

■ *Preheat oven to 300°F.*

Place beans in a 3-quart casserole. Stir in beer, catsup, onion, salt pork, brown sugar, molasses, dry mustard, Worcestershire sauce, and salt and pepper. Cover and place in preheated oven. Bake for about 4 hours or until beans are soft and quite thick, adding reserved bean cooking liquid as necessary during cooking time to keep beans from getting too dry.

Nestle frankfurters in beans and return to oven, uncovered. Cook for 30 minutes. Remove from oven and serve hot.

SWEDISH MEATBALLS

———

Serves 6.

1½	pounds lean ground beef or a combination of ¾ pound ground beef, ½ pound ground veal, and ¼ pound ground pork
1	cup fine bread crumbs
1	large egg
¼	cup minced fresh parsley
½	teaspoon freshly grated nutmeg (or to taste)
	Pinch allspice
	Salt to taste
	Pepper to taste
	Approximately 4 tablespoons butter
1	cup finely chopped onion
3	tablespoons all-purpose flour
2	cups warm beef stock
1	cup warm heavy cream

COMBINE MEAT, BREAD CRUMBS, EGG, 1 tablespoon parsley, nutmeg, allspice, and salt and pepper. Form into balls no more than 1 inch in diameter. Set aside.

Melt 2 tablespoons butter in a large sauté pan over medium-high heat. When melted, add onion. Sauté for about 3 minutes or until onion is just soft. Add meatballs, a few at a time, and fry, turning frequently, for about 5 minutes or until well browned. Drain on paper towels and continue to fry until all meatballs are browned, adding more butter if necessary.

When all meatballs are browned, stir flour into pan. Cook for about 2 minutes or until flour has absorbed all the fat. Whisk in beef stock. When well combined return meatballs to pan, add warm heavy cream and continue to cook for about 15 minutes or until meatballs are cooked and gravy is quite thick. Stir in remaining parsley and serve immediately with buttered noodles, if desired.

NOTE: Swedish Meatballs can be made in advance of use. Store either covered and refrigerated for up to two days or tightly sealed and frozen for up to three months.

CREAMED CHIPPED BEEF ON TOAST

Serves 6.

THE ARMY GAVE THIS TASTY SUPPER dish a bad name. Try it with green salad and a beer. It's delicious!

9	slices homemade-style white bread
1½	pounds dried beef
3	tablespoons unsalted butter or margarine
3	tablespoons all-purpose flour
2	cups warm milk
1	cup warm cream
	Salt to taste
	Pepper to taste
1	tablespoon minced fresh parsley

LIGHTLY TOAST BREAD. TRIM OFF crusts and slice in half diagonally. Set aside.

Separate beef into small pieces. If beef is very salty, let stand in boiling water to cover for 5 minutes. Drain off water and pat dry.

Melt butter in a heavy sauté pan over medium heat. When melted, add beef. Cook, stirring frequently, for about 5 minutes or until beef begins to crisp around the edges. Stir in flour. When flour is well absorbed, add warm milk and cream, stirring as you pour to keep lumps from forming. Allow to cook for about 3 minutes or until thick. Stir in salt and pepper.

Place three pieces of toast on each of six warm serving plates. Pour an equal portion of Chipped Beef over top. Serve immediately.

CHICKEN A LA KING

Serves 6.

9	pieces homemade-style white bread
2	tablespoons unsalted butter
1	cup sliced mushrooms
¼	cup minced celery
1	tablespoon minced onion
3	tablespoons all-purpose flour
1½	cups hot heavy cream or half-and-half
1	cup hot chicken stock
3	cups cooked chicken, diced
2	tablespoons minced fresh parsley
¼	cup chopped pimentos (optional)
2	large egg yolks
	Salt to taste
	Pepper to taste

TOAST BREAD. TRIM OFF CRUSTS AND cut in half diagonally. Set aside.

Melt 1 tablespoon butter in a heavy saucepan over medium heat. When melted, add mushrooms, celery, and onion. Sauté, stirring frequently, for about 6 minutes or until mushrooms have exuded most of their moisture and vegetables are soft. Add remaining butter. When melted, stir in flour until it has absorbed the fat. Pour in cream and chicken stock, whisking constantly. When well combined, add chicken, 1 tablespoon parsley, and pimentos, if using. Cook, stirring constantly, for about 4 minutes or until sauce begins to thicken.

Whisk a bit of the hot liquid into the egg yolks. Then whisk eggs into chicken mixture. Add salt and pepper and cook for an additional 5 minutes. Remove from heat.

Place three toast points on each of six warm serving plates. Place equal portions of Chicken à la King on top of each serving. Sprinkle with remaining parsley and serve immediately.

NOTE: Chicken à la King also may be served over rice or in commercially prepared puff pastry shells.

Creamy Chicken A La King served in a puff pastry shell and accompanied by a bed of greens.

LIVER AND ONIONS

Serves 6.

MY CHILDHOOD FAVORITE! PERHAPS because my mother cooked it so well, I have never suffered from the common liver-crinkle-nose syndrome. In fact, it is still one of my favorite dining-out meals.

¼ pound lean bacon slices
¼ cup all-purpose flour
    Salt to taste
    Pepper to taste
2   pounds calf's liver, thinly sliced
    Sautéed Onions*

PLACE BACON IN COLD, HEAVY FRYING pan over medium heat. When bacon begins to cook, lower heat. Fry, turning frequently, for about 10 minutes or until bacon is crisp. Place bacon on paper towels to drain. When well drained, crumble and set aside.

Pour off all but 1½ tablespoons fat from skillet. Reserve drained fat. Return pan to medium-high heat. Combine flour, salt, and pepper. Lightly dredge liver slices in seasoned flour. When bacon fat is hot, add liver slices. Raise heat to high and quickly sear for about 2 minutes. Then turn and brown other side for about 2 minutes. Do not overcook. Tender calf's liver should be served, at the most, medium-rare. Do not crowd pan when frying. If necessary, fry liver in batches, adding reserved bacon grease as necessary. Drain on paper towels. Serve covered with Sautéed Onions and sprinkle with crumbled bacon.

NOTE: You may eliminate bacon and fry liver in whatever fat you prefer. If using butter, add at least 1 teaspoon oil to keep from burning.

SAUTEED ONIONS

Makes approximately 2½ cups.

4   large red onions, peeled
2   tablespoons unsalted butter
    Salt to taste
    Pepper to taste
2   tablespoons brown sugar
1   teaspoon vinegar

SLICE ONIONS PAPER THIN. MELT butter in a large, heavy sauté pan over medium-high heat. When melted, add onions, salt, and pepper. Stir to coat. Cook, stirring frequently, for about 15 minutes or until onions soften and begin to brown. Stir in brown sugar and vinegar and continue to cook for 10 minutes or until onions begin to caramelize. Keep warm until ready to use.

SHRIMP WIGGLE

Serves 6.

EVERY FAMILY HAS A WIGGLE. OURS was usually tuna; shrimp was special! I'm sure that you will recognize this all-time American favorite.

4	tablespoons unsalted butter
1	cup chopped fresh mushrooms
2	tablespoons all-purpose flour
2	cups hot milk
½	pound Gouda or other mild cheese, grated
½	teaspoon paprika
2	cups cooked shrimp, diced
1	cup frozen petite peas, thawed
	Salt to taste
	Pepper to taste
¼	cup fresh bread crumbs
1	pound dried egg noodles

■ *Preheat oven to 350°F.*

GREASE 3-QUART CASSEROLE WITH 1 tablespoon butter and set aside.

Melt remaining butter in a heavy saucepan over medium heat. When hot, add mushrooms and sauté for 5 minutes or until very soft. Stir in flour and cook for 1 minute or until flour has absorbed all fat. Whisk in hot milk, cheese, and paprika. Cook, stirring constantly, for 5 minutes or until thick. Stir in shrimp, peas, and salt and pepper.

Cook noodles as directed on package. When cooked, drain well and combine with shrimp. Pour into prepared casserole and sprinkle with bread crumbs. Place in preheated oven and bake for 20 minutes or until bubbly. Serve immediately.

NOTE: Shrimp may be replaced with an equal portion of canned tuna or any other fresh fish, cooked chicken, turkey, or even cooked sausage meat.

MACARONI AND CHEESE

———

Serves 6.

THROUGH YEARS OF COOKING, A MAC-
aroni and Cheese disaster is the
most memorable. My family still
remembers the casserole filled with
hay and straw, or at least what
looked like hay and straw. I think I
have finally learned how to make
terrific Macaroni and Cheese.

4   tablespoons unsalted butter
3   tablespoons all-purpose flour
2   cups hot milk
1¼ cups grated American cheese
1¼ cups grated sharp cheddar
    cheese
    Salt to taste
    White pepper to taste
1   pound dried elbow macaroni

GREASE A 3-QUART CASSEROLE WITH
1 tablespoon butter. Melt remaining
butter in a medium saucepan over
high heat. When melted, add flour.
Cook, stirring constantly, for 1 minute or until flour has absorbed fat
and mixture is smooth. Whisk in
hot milk and cook, stirring constantly, for 3 minutes. Add 1 cup of
each cheese, and salt and pepper
and continue to cook, whisking
constantly, for 3 minutes or until
quite smooth.

Cook macaroni according to
package directions. Drain and rinse
under cold running water. Drain
well.

■ *Preheat oven to 400°F.*

Combine cheese sauce and macaroni and pour into prepared casserole. Combine remaining cheeses
and sprinkle on top of the casserole.
Place in preheated oven and bake
for 20 minutes or until casserole is
bubbly and top is light brown.
Serve immediately.

*Homestyle Macaroni and Cheese
garnished with fresh greens and
cherry tomatoes.*

MOM'S CHEESE CASSEROLE

——

Serves 6.

3   tablespoons unsalted butter
12 slices stale white bread
8   large eggs
1   tablespoon grated onion
3½ cups heavy cream or half-and-half
1   teaspoon light brown sugar
1   teaspoon dry mustard
1   teaspoon Worcestershire sauce
¼   teaspoon paprika
    Dash Tabasco™ sauce
    Salt to taste
    Pepper to taste
¾   pound grated sharp cheddar
    cheese
¾   pound grated Monterey jack
    cheese

GENEROUSLY BUTTER A 3-QUART casserole with 1 tablespoon butter. Set aside.

Cut crusts from bread and discard. Cut bread into small cubes. Melt remaining butter in a heavy sauté pan over medium heat. Add bread cubes and sauté, stirring constantly, for about 3 minutes or until bread has absorbed the butter. Remove from heat.

■ *Preheat oven to 350°F.*

Whisk together eggs, onion, cream, brown sugar, dry mustard, Worcestershire sauce, paprika, Tabasco™ sauce, and salt and pepper until well combined.

Combine the two cheeses. Place one-third of the bread cubes in the bottom of prepared casserole. Sprinkle with half of the cheese. Use half of the remaining bread cubes to make another layer on top of the cheese. Top with the remaining cheese, then with a final layer of bread cubes. Pour egg mixture over top and place in preheated oven. Bake for about 45 minutes or until casserole is bubbly and golden-brown. Serve immediately.

NOTE: This casserole may be put together early in the day and stored, covered and refrigerated, until ready to bake. If doing so, be sure to use a casserole that can go from the cold refrigerator to the heat of the oven.

CHEESE SOUFFLE

Serves 4.

4   tablespoons unsalted butter
2   tablespoons all-purpose flour
1   cup hot milk or half-and-half
¾   cup grated sharp cheddar cheese
     Tabasco™ sauce to taste
     Salt to taste
     White pepper to taste
4   large eggs, separated

GREASE A 2-QUART CASSEROLE WITH 1 tablespoon butter. Set aside.

Melt remaining butter in a heavy saucepan over medium heat. When melted, stir in flour. Cook, stirring constantly, for 1 minute or until mixture is smooth and well blended. Whisk in hot milk. Cook, whisking constantly, for about 4 minutes or until quite thick. Whisk in cheese, Tabasco™ sauce, and salt and white pepper, whisking constantly until cheese melts. Remove from heat and set aside to cool slightly.

Beat egg yolks until light yellow and very thick. Whisk a bit of the cheese mixture into the egg yolks, then whisk egg yolks back into the slightly cooled cheese mixture.

■ *Preheat oven to 375°F.*

Beat egg whites until stiff but not dry. Gently fold into the cheese mixture. Pour into prepared casserole. Place in preheated oven and bake for about 45 minutes or until golden-brown and puffed. Serve immediately.

NOTE: Do not open oven door for at least the first 30 minutes of baking or the soufflé will fall, never to rise again.

Hash Browns

Boiled Potatoes

Roasted Potatoes

Pan-fried Potatoes

Scalloped Potatoes

Mashed Potatoes

Baked Potatoes

French Fries

Potato Salad

Candied Sweet Potatoes

Potato Pancakes

Peas and Carrots

Creamed Spinach

Fried Green Tomatoes

Broiled Tomatoes

Old-fashioned Greens

Sauteed Creamed Cabbage

Red Cabbage

Corn Pudding

Succotash

Creamed Onions

Three-bean Salad

Pickled Beets

Coleslaw

Tossed Green Salad

4

POTATOES AND OTHER VEGETABLES

POTATOES AND VEGETABLES ARE MY favorite part of any meal. This is because my mother, unlike many cooks of her generation, did not boil our vegetables. She steamed them to capture their flavor and vitamins. (The only exception to this was her childhood favorite, green beans and potatoes with bacon, a delicious combination that turned into bland mush with hours of simmering.) She also used as many fresh vegetables as she could and we always began our meals with a raw salad.

Any potato or vegetable may be placed in a steamer basket over rapidly boiling water and steamed until just tender, a matter of minutes. Test for doneness by sticking the point of a sharp knife into the thickest part. If you want a crisp-tender vegetable, the knife should meet a bit of resistance. If you want a fully cooked, softer vegetable, the knife should easily pierce the thickest part. Toss with any amount of oil or butter, fresh herbs, and salt and/or pepper you desire. Or eat as is for almost no calories. Potatoes and vegetables may also be sliced,

coated with olive oil, seasoned with herbs and salt and pepper, and grilled over a hot fire until cooked to the desired degree of doneness. Use the knife test as for steamed.

I usually allow one medium to large potato per person with an extra one or two thrown in for seconds. The exception to this rule is for baked potatoes, where I use one large Idaho potato per person, and new potatoes where per person portion depends upon size. For tiny new red or yellow potatoes I allow at least three per person, always with extras for seconds.

HASH BROWNS

Serves 6.

1 recipe Boiled Potatoes*
2 tablespoons vegetable oil, butter, or margarine
   Salt to taste
   Pepper to taste
½ teaspoon paprika (optional)

CUT BOILED POTATOES INTO CUBES. Heat oil in a heavy sauté pan over medium-high heat. When hot, add potatoes, salt and pepper, and paprika. Press down with the back of a spatula to break up potatoes and press into hot fat. Lower heat to medium. Cover and cook for about 20 minutes or until bottom is brown and crusty. Carefully turn over in large chunks. Cover and fry for another 10 minutes or until brown. Serve hot.

VARIATION:
Add ¼ to ½ cup diced onion and/or ¼ cup diced red and/or green bell peppers, or 2 tablespoons chopped pimentos.

BOILED POTATOES

Serves 6.

6 to 8 medium-large russet or other all-purpose potatoes
   Water to cover
   Salt to taste
   Pepper to taste

PEEL POTATOES. AS YOU PEEL, PLACE in cool water to cover to prevent potatoes from discoloring. Cut into cubes, quarters, or whatever serving size you prefer. Place in a heavy saucepan with cool water to cover over high heat. Bring to a boil.

When boiling, lower heat to a simmer and simmer for 20 minutes or until tender but not mushy. Drain well.

Return to pan over low heat. Add salt and pepper to taste and gently shake pan for about 1 minute to dry potatoes. Serve immediately as is or with butter.

NOTE: New potatoes are cooked in the same fashion except that they should be well scrubbed and cooked in their skins.

VARIATIONS:
1. After draining, return potatoes to pan. Add 3 tablespoons melted butter and 1 tablespoon chopped fresh parsley or 1 tablespoon chopped fresh chives and salt and pepper to taste.
2. After draining, return potatoes to pan. Add ½ cup warm milk or heavy cream, 2 tablespoons butter, and salt and pepper to taste. Cook over low heat for about 5 minutes or until milk and seasonings are absorbed by potatoes.

ROASTED POTATOES

───

Serves 6.

6 to 8 all-purpose potatoes
⅓ cup olive or vegetable oil or melted
    butter
    Salt to taste
    Pepper to taste
    Paprika to taste (optional)

■ *Preheat oven to 400°F.*

PEEL POTATOES. AS YOU PEEL, PLACE in cool water to cover to prevent potatoes from discoloring. Cut into quarters. Pat dry.

Generously coat each quarter with oil. Place remaining oil in a small roasting pan. Add potatoes, sprinkle with salt and pepper and paprika, and place in preheated oven. Bake for about 30 minutes or until golden brown and crisp. Serve immediately.

PAN-FRIED POTATOES

───

Serves 6.

6 large all-purpose potatoes
3 tablespoons vegetable or olive oil,
    clarified butter, or bacon fat
¾ cup diced onion
    Salt to taste
    Pepper to taste
    Paprika to taste (optional)

PEEL POTATOES. AS YOU PEEL, PLACE in cool water to cover to prevent potatoes from discoloring.

Slice potatoes very thin or cut into ½-inch cubes. Place in a bowl of ice water and let stand for 30 minutes. Drain well and pat dry.

Heat oil in a large, heavy skillet over medium heat. When hot, add onions and fry for about 3 minutes. Add potatoes, cover, and lower heat.

Cook for about 20 minutes or until bottom is brown. Uncover potatoes and turn them, in as big chunks as possible, to the other side. Cover and fry for 15 minutes or until golden-brown. Serve immediately.

Alternate method: Do not cover potatoes. Fry over medium heat, stirring frequently, for about 30 minutes or until well browned. This version will give a crispier potato.

SCALLOPED POTATOES

━━━

Serves 6.

6 to 8 medium-to-large all-purpose potatoes

⅓ cup butter plus 2 tablespoons, melted

½ cup diced onion (optional)

Salt to taste

Pepper to taste

Approximately 3 tablespoons all-purpose flour

Approximately 2 cups warm milk or cream (or a combination of both)

¼ cup fine bread crumbs (optional)

■ *Preheat oven to 375°F.*

GENEROUSLY GREASE A 2-QUART CASserole and set aside.

Peel potatoes. As you peel, place in cool water to cover to prevent potatoes from discoloring. Pat potatoes dry and cut into very thin slices or use the slicing blade in a food processor.

Place a layer of potatoes on the bottom of prepared casserole. Sprinkle with onion, if using. Dot with butter and sprinkle with salt and pepper. Continue making layers of potatoes, dotting with butter, and sprinkling with flour, salt, and pepper until all potatoes are used. Add

warm milk to just the top layer of the potatoes. Do not cover. Sprinkle with bread crumbs and drizzle with melted butter.

Place in preheated oven. Bake for about 1 hour until knife inserted into the center meets no resistance. Serve hot.

VARIATIONS:

1. 1½ cups grated cheese of choice may be divided between the layers.
2. Any fresh or dried herb may be lightly sprinkled on each layer.
3. Minced, cooked ham or bacon can be sprinkled on each layer. If so, lessen salt considerably.

MASHED POTATOES

━━━

Serves 6.

THE BEST MASHED POTATOES ARE made by hand. However, if you choose to use an electric mixer, do not overwhip or potatoes will be starchy. Remember, leave those lumps!

6 to 8 russet potatoes or other all-
        purpose potatoes
        Water to cover
¼   cup butter or margarine
        Approximately ½ cup warm heavy
        cream or milk
        Salt to taste
        Pepper to taste

PEEL POTATOES. AS YOU PEEL, PLACE in cool water to cover to prevent potatoes from discoloring. Cut into cubes and place in a heavy saucepan with cool water to cover over high heat. Bring to a boil. When boiling, lower heat and simmer for 20 minutes or until potatoes are very soft and beginning to fall apart. Remove from heat and drain well.

Put drained potatoes through a potato ricer, food mill, or coarse sieve. Return to pan with remaining ingredients. Place over low heat and beat with a potato masher or wooden spoon until potatoes are quite fluffy and smooth.

Serve immediately as is or with butter or meat or chicken gravy (see pages 17 and 18).

VARIATIONS:
1. Stir in 1 tablespoon chopped fresh parsley, or 1 tablespoon chopped fresh chives, or ¼ cup grated cheese of choice after potatoes are mashed.
2. Place mashed potatoes in a buttered 1½-quart casserole. Pour ½ cup heavy cream over top. Sprinkle with ½ cup fine bread crumbs and ¼ cup grated Parmesan cheese. Place in a preheated 450°F oven and bake for about 10 minutes or until top is golden.
3. Leftover mashed potatoes make great potato cakes. Simply form into patties and fry in very hot clarified butter or vegetable or olive oil for about 4 minutes per side or until golden-brown.

Mashed Potatoes topped with melted butter. Real comfort food.

BAKED POTATOES

Serves 6.

6   large Idaho potatoes, free of
    blemishes
2   tablespoons vegetable oil
½   cup butter
    Salt to taste
    Pepper to taste

■ *Preheat oven to 400°F.*

SCRUB POTATOES WELL. PAT DRY. Generously coat skins with oil. Poke air holes in each potato using the tines of a kitchen fork. Place potatoes in preheated oven and bake for approximately 45 minutes or until knife inserted into the center meets no resistance. Immediately remove from oven.

Split open and season with butter and salt and pepper, if desired. Serve immediately.

VARIATIONS:
1. Baked potatoes may be eaten absolutely plain for a great diet filler-upper.
2. Any cheese, sour cream, or crème fraîche may be added to potato when it is split open. One to 2 tablespoons should be sufficient.
3. Fresh chives, parsley, scallions, or cooked onions also offer a tasty variation when sprinkled on top.

FRENCH FRIES

Serves 6.

THERE IS NOTHING TASTIER THAN A homemade French fry. The secret of making great ones is ice-cold potatoes tossed in very hot oil at the perfect temperature.

6   large Idaho potatoes
    Approximately 6 cups vegetable oil
    Salt to taste
    Pepper to taste

PEEL POTATOES. AS YOU PEEL, PLACE in cool water to cover to prevent potatoes from discoloring.

Cut potatoes into strips of any size you desire and immediately place in a bowl of ice water. Allow to soak for at least 30 minutes.

Place oil in a deep-fat fryer with a basket over high heat. Bring to 375°F on a food thermometer. Remove potato strips from ice water, a few at a time. Pat very dry. When dried, place in hot fat and fry, shaking basket from time to time, for about 3 minutes or until cooked and golden-brown. Drain onto paper towels. Sprinkle with salt and pepper and serve immediately.

NOTE: If you want to make a batch of French fries before serving, the potatoes might get soft. If so, return them to the hot fat for about 1 minute to recrisp.

Potato Salad

━━━

Serves 6.

A sure sign that summer has arrived is my first bowl of potato salad. Everyone has a favorite recipe. This is mine: Plain old-fashioned Potato Salad that makes enough for leftovers.

8 large all-purpose potatoes
4 hard-boiled eggs
1 cup diced celery
½ cup chopped scallions
½ cup diced onion
½ teaspoon celery seed
¼ teaspoon dry mustard
1 to 2 cups mayonnaise (or to taste)
   Salt to taste
   Pepper to taste

SCRUB POTATOES WELL. PLACE IN water in a large saucepan over medium-high heat. Bring to a boil. Boil for about 30 minutes or until tender. Drain well.

Cool until able to handle. Peel and cut into 1- to 1¼-inch chunks. Place in a large mixing bowl.

Peel and chop eggs. Add to potatoes with celery, scallions, and onion. Toss to combine. Stir celery seed and dry mustard into mayonnaise. When well combined, fold into potatoes, being careful not to mash the vegetables. Cover and refrigerate for at least 2 hours before serving.

Candied Sweet Potatoes

━━━

Serves 6.

SWEET POTATOES MAY BE COOKED BY any method used for white potatoes. However, they are best known for their appearance in the candied guise on the holiday dinner table.

6 medium sweet potatoes
⅓ cup butter
½ cup light brown sugar
½ teaspoon ground cinnamon

PEEL POTATOES. PLACE IN COOL WA-ter to cover in a medium saucepan over high heat. Bring to a boil, and boil for about 20 minutes or until just tender. Drain well.

Cut into ½-inch slices and place in a buttered 2-quart baking dish.

■ *Preheat oven to 300°F.*

Melt butter in a small saucepan over low heat. When melted, add sugar and cinnamon and cook for 3 minutes. Pour over potatoes and place in preheated oven. Bake, turn-ing occasionally, for about 30 minutes or until well glazed. Serve hot.

NOTE: Also familiar are marshmallow-topped sweet potatoes. For these, make mashed sweet potatoes following the directions for regular mashed potatoes on page 72. Stir in ½ teaspoon ground cinnamon and place in a buttered 2-quart casserole. Cover top with marshmallows and bake for about 15 minutes or until heated through and marshmallows are melted and lightly brown.

POTATO PANCAKES

Serves 6.

6   medium all-purpose potatoes
1   cup grated onion
2   large eggs
1   tablespoon all-purpose flour
⅛   teaspoon baking powder
    Salt to taste
    Pepper to taste
    Approximately ¼ cup vegetable
    oil, clarified butter, or other oil of
    choice

PEEL POTATOES. AS YOU PEEL, PLACE in cool water to cover to prevent potatoes from discoloring.

Combine onion, eggs, flour, baking powder, and salt and pepper.

Drain potatoes and pat dry. Grate potatoes in a food processor fitted with the shredding blade or by hand on the larger side of a hand-held grater. When all potatoes are grated, squeeze out liquid and drain it off. When well drained, combine grated potato with egg mixture.

Heat 1 tablespoon oil in a heavy skillet over medium-high heat. When hot, add potato batter by the serving spoonful. Lower heat to medium and fry for about 3 minutes per side or until golden-brown. Drain on paper towels and keep warm. Continue frying, using 1 tablespoon oil at a time, until all potato batter is used. Serve hot.

NOTE: You can serve potato pancakes with applesauce, sliced fruit, sour cream, or gravy. Delete the onion and you can also serve them with jelly and syrup.

Crispy Potato Pancakes with a fresh fruit garnish and a dollop of sour cream topped by chives.

PEAS AND CARROTS

Serves 6.

I NOW MOST OFTEN USE FROZEN PE-
tite peas, since fresh, tender peas
are so infrequently available. They
are almost as good.

4   carrots, peeled
1   package frozen petite peas
1   tablespoon butter (optional)
     Salt to taste
     Pepper to taste

CUT CARROTS INTO SMALL CUBES
equivalent to the size of the peas.
Place in cold water to cover in a
medium-sized saucepan and bring
to a boil over medium heat (or in
top half of a steamer over boiling
water). When boiling, lower heat to
a simmer and cook for 3 minutes or
until just tender. Add peas and
again bring to a boil. When boiling,
remove from heat and drain immediately. When drained, add butter
and salt and pepper and serve immediately.

CREAMED SPINACH

Serves 6.

2   pounds leaf spinach (or 2 boxes
     frozen spinach, thawed)
2   tablespoons butter
½   cup heavy cream
     Dash freshly ground nutmeg
     Salt to taste
     Pepper to taste

TRIM ALL WILTED LEAVES AND TOUGH
stems from spinach. Place in warm
water to cover and toss vigorously.
Drain and repeat. Rinse at least two
more times in cold water or as many
times as necessary until all sand
disappears.

Place the rinsed spinach in a
large saucepan. Cover and place
over low heat. Cook for about 4
minutes or until all spinach is wilted
and tender. You will not need to
add more liquid.

When spinach is tender, drain
well. Squeeze out all excess liquid.
Chop in food processor fitted with
a metal blade or by hand with a
large, sharp chef's knife. Place in a
saucepan with remaining ingredients over medium heat. Cook, stirring frequently, for about 5 minutes
or until cream has reduced and
thickened. Serve immediately.

FRIED GREEN TOMATOES

━━

Serves 6.

GREEN TOMATOES ARE A SURE SIGN of summer's bounty. When the tomato crop gets to be too much to handle, green ones get picked before they can ripen. You can also fry ripe tomatoes, but they must be quite firm.

5   large green tomatoes
2   large eggs
½   cup milk
    Tabasco™ sauce to taste
1   cup all-purpose flour
¼   cup cornmeal
    Salt to taste
    Pepper to taste
¼   cup clarified butter or oil of choice

WASH TOMATOES AND PAT DRY. CORE and cut crosswise into ½-inch slices.

Whisk eggs, milk, and Tabasco™ sauce together and pour into a shallow bowl.

Combine flour, cornmeal, and salt and pepper, and pour onto a plate.

Heat butter in a heavy sauté pan over medium heat. When hot, dip tomato slices in egg mixture, then in flour. Shake off excess and place in sauté pan. Fry for about 3 minutes per side or until golden-brown. Drain on paper towels and serve immediately.

VARIATION:
Sprinkle each side of the tomato slices with about ¼ teaspoon light brown sugar before frying. When all tomatoes are fried, remove them from pan and stir 1 cup heavy cream into pan; cook for about 4 minutes or until quite thick. Pour over tomatoes and serve immediately.

BROILED TOMATOES

━━

Serves 6.

6   ripe tomatoes
2   tablespoons fine bread crumbs
2   tablespoons melted butter
    Salt to taste
    Pepper to taste

■ *Preheat broiler.*

WASH AND DRY TOMATOES. CUT IN half crosswise. Place on broiler pan and sprinkle tops of each half with bread crumbs, drizzle with butter, and season with salt and pepper. Place in preheated broiler for about 4 minutes or until bubbly and golden-brown. Serve immediately, allowing two halves per person.

NOTE: You also may add ½ teaspoon grated Parmesan cheese to each top as well as a sprinkling of any fresh or dried herb you like.

OLD-FASHIONED GREENS

Serves 6.

GREENS CAN MEAN ANY GREEN, LEAFY vegetable. Cultivated greens include spinach, kale, chard, mustard, beet, collard, and turnip greens. Wild greens include dandelion, poke sallet, and creasy. Methods of cooking depend on the region and culture. Here is a simple version with some regional variations.

3	pounds fresh greens
½	pound lean bacon
½	cup water
2	tablespoons cider vinegar
¼	teaspoon crushed red pepper flakes or 1 dried red peppercorn
	Salt to taste
	Pepper to taste

WASH AND TRIM GREENS AS DIRECTED for spinach on page 78. If leaves are very large (such as with collard), fold and cut into pieces.

Place bacon in a large saucepan over medium heat. Fry, turning frequently, for about 4 minutes or until cooked but not crisp. Place greens on top of bacon with the fat. Add water, cider vinegar, and red pepper flakes. Cover and cook for 5 to 20 minutes, depending on greens. Very fresh tender greens take much less time than coarse greens such as collard and kale.

When greens are tender, taste and adjust seasoning. Add salt and pepper if necessary. Drain off and reserve liquid. Serve greens with corn bread (see page 92) and reserved pot liquor on the side.

VARIATIONS:
1. Replace bacon with ham hock, salt pork, or any other smoked meat.
2. Add chopped onions and potatoes, allowing 1 large onion and about 4 medium potatoes.
3. Serve cooked greens topped with 1 cup chopped red onion.

SAUTÉED CREAMED CABBAGE

Serves 6.

1   1½-pound firm head green cabbage
2   tablespoons butter
1   teaspoon light brown sugar
    Salt to taste
    Pepper to taste
½   cup heavy cream

CORE AND WASH CABBAGE. ALLOW to drain. Shred cabbage in a food processor fitted with the shredder blade, or by hand using a sharp chef's knife.

Melt butter in a large sauté pan over medium heat. When melted, add cabbage, brown sugar, and salt and pepper. Cover and allow to cook for about 6 minutes or until cabbage is crisp-tender. Add heavy cream and cook for another 2 minutes. Serve immediately.

RED CABBAGE

Serves 6.

I WAS TAUGHT TO MAKE RED CABBAGE by a third-generation German-American painter. His mother had taught him to make it so he could take a bit of home with him when he went off to the big city.

1   1½-pound firm head red cabbage
2   Granny Smith apples
2   tablespoons melted pork fat or oil of choice
3   tablespoons apple cider
2   tablespoons cider vinegar
¼   cup brown sugar
1   tablespoon all-purpose flour
    Salt to taste
    Pepper to taste

CORE AND WASH CABBAGE. DRAIN well. Shred in food processor fitted with the shredder blade, or by hand using a sharp chef's knife.

Peel and core apples. Shred, using the same method as above. Combine cabbage and apples.

Heat fat in a deep saucepan over medium-high heat. When hot, add cabbage-apple mixture. Stir in apple cider. Cover, lower heat, and cook for about 15 minutes. Stir in vinegar, sugar, flour, and salt and pepper. When well combined, cover and cook for an additional 10 minutes or until cabbage is very tender, sauce is thick, and flavors are well balanced. Serve immediately.

CORN PUDDING

Serves 6.

3	large eggs
2	cups cooked fresh corn kernels (frozen or canned may be substituted)
¼	cup melted unsalted butter
2	tablespoons all-purpose flour
1	tablespoon grated onion
¼	teaspoon Tabasco™ sauce (or to taste)
1	cup hot milk
	Salt to taste
	Pepper to taste

■ *Preheat oven to 350°F.*

GENEROUSLY BUTTER A 1½-QUART baking dish or casserole and set aside.

Separate eggs. Beat whites until stiff but not dry.

Combine egg yolks, corn, butter, flour, grated onion, and Tabasco™ sauce. When well blended, stir in hot milk and salt and pepper. When mixed, fold in beaten egg whites.

Pour into prepared baking dish or casserole and place in preheated oven. Bake for 45 minutes or until pudding is just set and gently browned on top. Serve hot from baking dish.

SUCCOTASH

Serves 6.

THIS SEEMS TO BE ABOUT THE EARLIest American vegetable recipe combining our native beans and corn. A great summer favorite with fresh beans and corn, it is almost as good made from frozen vegetables in the winter.

2	cups fresh baby lima beans
1	2-ounce piece salt pork
¼	cup water
½	teaspoon sugar
	Salt to taste
	Pepper to taste
2	cups fresh corn kernels
½	cup heavy cream

PLACE LIMA BEANS, SALT PORK, WAter, and salt and pepper in a heavy saucepan over medium heat. Bring to a boil. When boiling, lower heat to a simmer and cook for about 5 minutes or until beans are tender. Add corn and cream and cook for 5 minutes or until slightly thickened. Serve immediately.

Succulent Succotash.

CREAMED ONIONS

———   *Serves 6.*

TO SAVE TIME AND ENERGY YOU CAN use frozen pearl onions in this recipe. If you do so, make sure you drain them well, otherwise your cream sauce will be runny.

2	pounds pearl onions
2	tablespoons butter
2	tablespoons all-purpose flour
½	cup warm heavy cream
½	cup warm milk
	Dash freshly ground nutmeg
	Salt to taste
	White pepper to taste
2	egg yolks, beaten

TRIM ROOT END FROM ONION AND cut a shallow cross into it. Place onions in rapidly boiling salted water for 1 minute. Remove from heat and let stand 1 minute. Drain and pop onions from skins. Place peeled onion in about 1 inch cool water in a medium-sized saucepan over medium heat. Bring to a boil. When boiling, lower heat and simmer for about 10 minutes or until onions are tender. Drain well.

Melt butter in same saucepan over low heat. When melted, stir in flour. When well blended, whisk in cream, milk, nutmeg, and salt and white pepper. Stirring constantly, cook for about 3 minutes or until well blended and slightly thick. Whisk a bit of the hot sauce into the beaten eggs, then whisk the eggs back into the sauce. Cook, stirring constantly, for about 3 minutes. Add onions and continue to cook for another 3 minutes. Remove from heat and serve immediately.

THREE-BEAN SALAD

———   *Serves 6.*

2	cups cooked red kidney beans
2	cups cooked, cut, green or wax beans
2	cups cooked chick-peas
1	cup diced red onion
2	tablespoons sweet pickle relish
1	clove garlic, peeled and minced
1	tablespoon sweet mustard (honey or German)
½	cup cider vinegar
1	tablespoon vegetable oil
	Salt to taste
	Pepper to taste

COMBINE ALL INGREDIENTS. COVER and refrigerate for at least 1 hour. Taste and adjust seasoning before serving.

Three-Bean Salad dressed with fresh parsley.

PICKLED BEETS

▬▬▬▬   *Serves 6.*

2   bunches fresh beets
1   large red onion
1   cup cider vinegar
2   tablespoons sugar
¼   teaspoon caraway seeds (optional)
    Salt to taste
    Pepper to taste

WASH BEETS. TRIM OFF ALL BUT 1 inch of the stem end. Place in a heavy saucepan with cool water to cover over high heat. Bring to a boil. When boiling, lower heat and simmer for about 30 minutes or until a knife inserted into the center of a beet meets no resistance. Drain and rinse beets under cold running water. Allow to cool until able to handle.

Trim off tops and slip off skin. Cut crosswise into thin slices. Place in a nonreactive container. Peel onion and cut crosswise into thin slices. Pull slices apart into rings. Add to beets.

Toss beets and onions with remaining ingredients. Cover and allow to stand for at least 2 hours before serving. It will keep, covered and refrigerated, for at least a week.

COLESLAW

▬▬▬▬   *Serves 4 to 6.*

1   2-pound firm head green
    cabbage
1   large carrot, peeled
½   teaspoon poppy seeds or celery
    seeds
½   cup mayonnaise
½   cup sour cream
1   tablespoon fresh lemon juice
1   tablespoon sugar
½   teaspoon dry mustard
    Salt to taste
    Pepper to taste

CORE AND WASH CABBAGE. DRAIN well. Shred in a food processor fitted with the shredder blade, or by hand using a sharp chef's knife. Grate carrot in the same fashion or on the coarse side of a hand-held grater.

Place cabbage and carrots in a nonreactive container. Combine remaining ingredients. When well combined, pour over cabbage and carrots and toss to coat. Serve immediately.

Tossed Green Salad

THE PERFECT TOSSED GREEN SALAD IS
not iceberg lettuce, carton tomatoes,
and commercially bottled dressing.
It is a subtle blend of soft and crisp
lettuces mixed with sweet and bitter
greens, tossed with a nicely balanced homemade dressing. You
can, if you like, add ripe tomatoes
and tender fresh vegetables.

Some of the salad makings now
available are red or green leaf, Bos-
ton, romaine, and Bibb lettuces,
dandelion greens, mâche (or lamb's
tongue), chicory (frisée), arugula,
watercress, endive, fennel, radic-
chio, and spinach. Use them all
and throw in some edible flowers
for color and fragrance. A basic
homemade salad dressing is three to
four parts oil (olive, peanut, or other
vegetable oil, one type or blended,
often used in combination with a
small amount of walnut, sesame, or
other intensely flavored oil) to one
part vinegar (various wines or cham-
pagne, balsamic, or fruit-flavored)
or lemon juice, seasoned with salt
and pepper. You might also add
Dijon mustard (no more than 2
teaspoons per cup of dressing) and/
or minced fresh herbs to taste.

BAKING POWDER BISCUITS

POPOVERS

MOM'S ROLLS

CORN BREAD

QUICK CINNAMON COFFEE CAKE

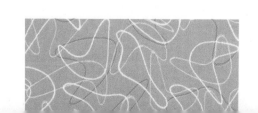

5

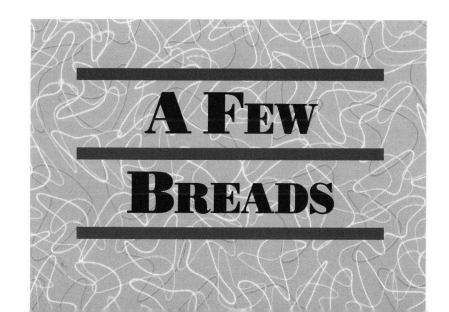

A FEW
BREADS

BAKING POWDER BISCUITS

▬

*Makes approximately
1 dozen biscuits.*

THESE ARE PERHAPS MY FAMILY'S FA-
vorite morning food. I've made so
many I believe that I have a fail-
safe, quick method.

2¼ cups all-purpose flour
1 tablespoon fine cornmeal
4 teaspoons baking powder
1 teaspoon sugar (or to taste), or salt
   to taste
⅓ cup solid vegetable shortening
   Approximately ⅔ cup milk
1 tablespoon butter or margarine

■ *Preheat oven to 450°F.*

PLACE FLOUR, CORNMEAL, BAKING
powder, and sugar or salt in food
processor fitted with the metal
blade. Use quick on-and-off turns
to combine. Add shortening and
again use quick on-and-off turns to
just combine. With motor running,
add milk and process quickly to
make a soft dough.

Turn out onto a lightly floured
board. Pat down and smooth edges
to form a circle about ¾-inch thick.
Cut out circles using a 2-inch biscuit
cutter or a drinking glass with a 2-
inch opening.

Place butter or margarine in a
cast-iron skillet or baking pan. Place
in preheated oven and allow to melt.
When butter is melted and pan is
hot, place biscuits into pan with all
sides touching. Return to oven and
bake for about 12 minutes or until
lightly brown and slightly risen.
Serve hot.

POPOVERS

▬*Makes up to 10, depending on size.*

1 cup all-purpose flour
½ teaspoon salt (or to taste)
½ teaspoon sugar
2 large eggs
1 cup milk
2 tablespoons melted unsalted butter
3 tablespoons salted butter

**An assortment of fresh-baked bread:
Baking Powder Biscuits, Popovers,
Mom's Rolls, and Corn Bread.**

■ *Preheat oven to 450°F.*

COMBINE FLOUR, SALT, SUGAR, EGGS,
milk, and melted butter in blender
and process until very smooth.

With remaining butter, generously grease popover or muffin pans
or custard cups. Place in preheated
oven for about 2 minutes to heat.
When very hot, fill each cup about
two-thirds full with batter. Place in
oven and bake for 30 minutes.
Lower heat and bake for an additional 15 minutes or until crusty,
golden-brown, and well risen. Do
not open oven for first 30 minutes
or popovers will not rise properly.
Serve immediately.

VARIATIONS:
1. Add 3 tablespoons grated cheese.
2. Add 3 tablespoons chopped
cooked ham or bacon.
3. Add 2 tablespoons minced fresh
chives or 1 tablespoon minced fresh
herb of choice.

MOM'S ROLLS

▬▬ *Makes approximately 2 dozen rolls.*

WHEN I WAS A CHILD THESE ROLLS were our white bread. In later years they were weekend and holiday treats

1	package yeast
½	cup warm water
1	cup Mashed Potatoes*
¾	cup vegetable shortening
7	cups all-purpose flour
¼	cup sugar
1	tablespoon salt (or to taste)
2	large eggs, beaten
1	cup warm milk
	Approximately ½ cup softened butter

DISSOLVE THE YEAST IN WARM WATER. Combine potatoes, shortening, 1 cup flour, sugar, and salt. When well combined, add dissolved yeast. Beat in eggs, milk, and remaining flour. When well beaten, cover and let rest in a warm spot for 2 hours.

Roll out on a lightly floured board to about ½-inch thick. Cut out circles with a 2-inch biscuit cutter. Brush the top of one circle with softened butter. Place another circle on top and pinch edges together. Generously butter two 8-inch-square baking pans. Place rolls next to one another in prepared pans. Cover and let rise away from drafts for about 2 hours.

■ *Preheat oven to 375°F.*

Place rolls in preheated oven and bake for about 20 minutes or until golden-brown. Serve hot.

CORN BREAD

▬▬ *Serves 6.*

1	cup all-purpose flour
1	cup yellow cornmeal
4	teaspoons baking powder
1	teaspoon sugar (optional)
¼	teaspoon salt (or to taste)
1	large egg, beaten
1	cup milk
2	tablespoons melted unsalted butter
2	tablespoons salted butter

■ *Preheat oven to 450°F.*

COMBINE FLOUR, CORNMEAL, BAKING powder, sugar, and salt. Stir in egg, milk, and melted butter until just combined. Put remaining butter in an 8-inch-square baking pan and place in preheated oven for 2 minutes. When butter is melted and pan is hot, pour in corn bread batter and return to oven. Bake for approximately 25 minutes or until golden-brown. Serve hot.

VARIATIONS:
1. Muffins and corn sticks can be made by placing this batter in muffin tins or corn stick pans.
2. Buttermilk may replace the whole milk.
3. Bacon fat may replace butter. If doing so, cook enough bacon to crumble at least three or four strips into the batter.
4. One cup cooked corn kernels, a dash of Tabasco™ sauce, and a minced jalapeño pepper can be added to the batter.
5. Add ½ cup grated sharp cheddar cheese to batter.

QUICK CINNAMON COFFEE CAKE

Makes one 9-inch cake.

THIS COFFEE CAKE IS SIMPLE TO MAKE and it fills the morning air with a delectable cinnamon smell.

6   tablespoons unsalted butter
1   cup sugar
2   large eggs
2   cups sifted all-purpose flour
1½ teaspoons baking powder
¼   teaspoon salt
2   teaspoons ground cinnamon
1   cup milk
1   cup fresh blueberries or other chopped fresh fruit (optional)
    Crumb Topping*

■ *Preheat oven to 350° F.*

GREASE AND FLOUR A 9-INCH-ROUND cake pan and set aside.

Beat butter and sugar until light and fluffy. Add eggs and beat to combine. Combine dry ingredients and add to creamed mixture alternately with milk. Beat until just combined. Pour mixture into prepared pan and top with fresh fruit if using and Crumb Topping. Place in preheated oven and bake for about 30 minutes or until cake tester inserted into center comes out clean. Serve warm.

CRUMB TOPPING

Makes approximately 1½ cups.

1   cup chopped walnuts or other nuts
½   cup light brown sugar
2   tablespoons all-purpose flour
2   teaspoons ground cinnamon
2   tablespoons chilled butter

COMBINE ALL INGREDIENTS. WORK butter into the mixture with fingers until crumbly. Use as directed as a cake topping.

DEVIL'S FOOD CAKE

PINEAPPLE UPSIDE-DOWN CAKE

BROWN SUGAR POUND CAKE

ORANGE CAKE

JELLY ROLL

GINGERBREAD

RICE PUDDING

BERRY/FRUIT COBBLER

FRESH COCONUT CAKE

STRAWBERRY SHORTCAKE

ANGEL FOOD CAKE

CHOCOLATE CREAM PIE

CHOCOLATE PUDDING

DEVIL'S FLOAT

BREAD PUDDING

CUSTARD

FLOATING ISLAND

BASIC CUPCAKES

FRUIT PIES

VANILLA ICE CREAM

BROWNIES

LEMON MERINGUE PIE

SCHAUM TORTE

OATMEAL COOKIES

CHOCOLATE-CHIP COOKIES

SUGAR COOKIES

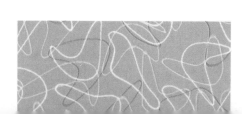

6

CAKES, PUDDINGS, AND OTHER SWEETS

DEVIL'S FOOD CAKE

Makes one 8-inch 3-layer cake.

THIS WAS MY CHILDHOOD FAVORITE and it still remains one of my favorite cakes.

¾   cup unsalted butter
1   cup white sugar
½   cup light brown sugar
3   large eggs
1   teaspoon pure vanilla extract
2½   cups all-purpose flour
½   cup cocoa
1½   teaspoons baking soda
¼   teaspoon salt
1½   cups sour milk
      Quick Seven-Minute Frosting*

■ *Preheat oven to 325°F.*

SPRAY THREE 8-INCH-ROUND CAKE pans with nonstick spray (or grease and flour them). Set aside.

Cream butter and sugars until light and fluffy. Beat in eggs one at a time. Add vanilla. Sift together all dry ingredients. Add to the creamed mixture alternately with sour milk. When well combined, pour into prepared pans and place in preheated oven. Bake for 25 minutes or until cake tester inserted into center comes out clean.

Remove from oven and let stand 5 minutes. Then turn out on wire cake racks to cool. When cool, place one layer on a cake plate. Coat with Quick Seven-Minute Frosting. Top with second layer and spread on frosting. Top with final layer and completely cover cake with remaining frosting. Do not refrigerate or frosting will get sticky.

NOTE: Make sour milk by adding 1 teaspoon white vinegar or lemon juice to milk and allowing it to sit for 10 minutes.

QUICK SEVEN-MINUTE FROSTING

Makes enough to frost one 8-inch cake.

REAL SEVEN-MINUTE FROSTING IS delicious but it is time-consuming and doesn't always work. This is a fail-safe version.

3   large egg whites
¼   teaspoon salt
⅜   cup sugar
1⅛ cups white Karo® syrup
2   teaspoons pure vanilla extract

USING AN ELECTRIC MIXER, BEAT EGG whites with salt until fluffy. Add sugar and beat until glossy. Add Karo syrup and vanilla and beat until frosting is glossy and holds a stiff peak. Use immediately.

PINEAPPLE UPSIDE-DOWN CAKE

Makes one 9-inch-square or one 9-inch-round cake.

PINEAPPLE UPSIDE-DOWN CAKE IS often baked in a cast-iron skillet, but you can also use a 9-inch-square cake pan or a 9-inch by 2-inch round baking dish.

¼   cup unsalted butter
1   cup light brown sugar
     Approximately 7 canned pineapple rings, well drained
7   candied or maraschino cherries (optional)
½   cup walnut halves
3   large eggs, separated
1½   cups sugar
1   teaspoon pure vanilla extract
1½   cups sifted all-purpose flour
1½   teaspoons baking powder
½   cup water

■ *Preheat oven to 350°F.*

MELT BUTTER IN A CAST-IRON SKILLET over low heat. When melted, stir in brown sugar. When well combined, quickly place whole pineapple rings on the bottom in a neat pattern. Place a cherry in the center of each ring, if using, and place walnut meats in any empty spaces. Set aside, but keep warm.

Beat egg yolks and sugar until thick and lemon-colored. Stir in vanilla. Sift flour and baking powder together and add to egg yolks alternately with water.

Beat egg whites until stiff peaks form, then fold into the egg yolk batter. Pour into the prepared pan and place in preheated oven. Bake for 30 minutes or until golden-brown. Place on wire rack to cool for 10 minutes, then invert onto a serving plate. Serve with heavy cream, if desired.

NOTE: Any fruit may be substituted for the pineapple in this recipe.

Brown Sugar Pound Cake

■ *Makes one 10-inch tube cake or two 8½-inch by 4½-inch by 2½-inch loaf cakes.*

Pound cakes are the all-time great keepers. They also freeze well. Keep one on hand at all times for quick desserts with fresh fruit, whipped cream, or any dessert sauce.

2   cups unsalted butter or margarine
2½   cups brown sugar
1   tablespoon freshly grated orange rind
1½   teaspoons pure vanilla extract
10   large eggs
4½   cups sifted cake flour
½   teaspoon ground mace
¼   teaspoon salt

■ *Preheat oven to 325°F.*

Grease and flour pan and set aside.

Beat butter until light and fluffy. Add sugar and beat until very smooth. Mix in orange rind and vanilla. When well combined, beat in eggs, one at a time, until well blended.

Sift dry ingredients together three times, then sift into batter ½ cup at a time. When well combined, pour into prepared pan and place in preheated oven. Bake for 20 minutes, then raise heat to 350°F and bake for 40 minutes or until the crack down the center is golden-brown and a cake tester inserted in the center comes out clean.

Remove from oven. Cool on wire cake racks for 5 minutes, then invert pans onto racks and remove cake. Allow to cool before cutting.

NOTE: Pound cake may be wrapped in plastic wrap or aluminum foil and stored in the refrigerator for up to one week. It can be frozen, tightly wrapped, for up to six months.

ORANGE CAKE

Makes one 10-inch cake.

7   large eggs, separated
1   cup superfine sugar
5   tablespoons fresh orange juice
2   tablespoons freshly grated orange
    rind
1   cup sifted flour
    Pinch salt
1   teaspoon cream of tartar
    Orange Glaze*

■ *Preheat oven to 325°F.*

BEAT EGG YOLKS AND ½ CUP SUGAR until thick and lemon-colored. Stir in orange juice and orange rind.

Sift flour over egg yolk mixture, a bit at a time, and gently fold to combine. Beat egg whites until foamy. Add salt and cream of tartar and beat until soft peaks form. Add remaining sugar and beat until stiff peaks form.

Gently fold egg yolk mixture into egg whites and pour into an ungreased, 10-inch tube pan with removable bottom. Run a kitchen knife through the batter to allow air to escape. Place in preheated oven and bake for about 1 hour or until cake tester inserted in the center comes out clean.

When cake is done, invert on a wire cake rack and cool in pan. When completely cool, turn cake right side up and gently run a sharp knife around the edges and lift cake from the pan, holding on to the tube. Slowly and carefully run knife around tube and between cake and bottom. Invert cake onto cake plate and tap it free. Brush with Orange Glaze.

ORANGE GLAZE

*Makes enough for one
10-inch cake.*

1   cup sifted confectioner's sugar
2½ teaspoons fresh orange juice
1   teaspoon freshly grated orange
    rind

COMBINE ALL INGREDIENTS AND STIR until very smooth. Use as directed.

JELLY ROLL

▬

Serves 8 to 10.

2 tablespoons unsalted butter
3 large eggs
1 cup superfine sugar
3 tablespoons cold water
1 teaspoon pure vanilla extract
1 cup sifted all-purpose flour
1 teaspoon baking powder
⅛ teaspoon salt
   Approximately ½ cup
   confectioner's sugar
¾ to 1 cup jelly or jam

■ *Preheat oven to 375°F.*

GENEROUSLY GREASE A 15-INCH JELLY roll pan. Line with parchment or wax paper. Butter and flour the paper and set aside.

Beat eggs until very light yellow. Gradually beat in sugar. When well combined, add water and vanilla.

Sift together flour, baking powder, and salt, and quickly beat into the egg mixture until smooth. Pour into prepared pan and place in preheated oven. Bake for 15 minutes or until a cake tester inserted in the center comes out clean.

Immediately turn out onto a clean kitchen towel that has been dusted with confectioner's sugar. Peel off paper and trim off crisp edges. Roll the cake up in the towel lengthwise and let rest for 3 minutes. Unroll and let stand, then reroll and let stand until cool. When cool, unwrap and coat with jelly. Roll cake lengthwise without the towel into a neat roll. Place on serving platter and dust with confectioner's sugar.

This Jelly Roll was dusted with confectioner's sugar to create a triangular pattern.

GINGERBREAD

■ *Makes one 13-inch by 9-inch by 2-inch cake.*

1   cup unsalted butter or margarine
1   cup light brown sugar
1   cup molasses
2   large eggs
1   cup sour milk (see page 96)
3   cups all-purpose flour
1   teaspoon baking soda
1½ teaspoons ground ginger
1   teaspoon ground cinnamon
½   teaspoon ground mace
½   teaspoon ground cloves
    Chantilly Cream*

■ *Preheat oven to 350°F.*

LIGHTLY GREASE AND FLOUR A 13-inch by 9-inch by 2-inch cake pan. Place the butter, brown sugar, and molasses in a medium-sized saucepan over low heat. Cook, stirring constantly, for about 10 minutes or until butter has melted and sugar has dissolved. Remove from heat and allow to cool slightly.

Beat the eggs until light. Stir in sour milk, then cooled butter mixture. Sift dry ingredients together two times, then add to liquid mixture, ½ cup at a time, beating well after each incorporation.

When well blended, pour in prepared cake pan and place in preheated oven. Bake for 40 minutes or until a cake tester inserted in the center comes out clean. Remove from oven and let stand for 10 minutes. Cut into serving pieces and serve each slice with a generous portion of Chantilly Cream.

CHANTILLY CREAM

■ *Makes approximately 1 cup.*

CHANTILLY CREAM IS JUST A FANCY name for whipped cream. However, my mother said Chantilly Cream was softly whipped cream and more elegant than the plain old whipped stuff.

1   cup very cold heavy cream
3   tablespoons confectioner's sugar
½   teaspoon pure vanilla extract

BEAT HEAVY CREAM SLIGHTLY. ADD sugar and vanilla and beat until it holds its shape but doesn't form stiff peaks. Serve immediately.

RICE PUDDING

Serves 6.

RICE PUDDING HAS ALWAYS BEEN MY nemesis. It's either too dry, too runny, not sweet enough, etc. I hope this recipe is the final attempt.

1   tablespoon unsalted butter
½   cup white or brown rice
4   cups milk
¾   cup sugar (or to taste)
    Dash salt
1   teaspoon pure vanilla extract
¼   teaspoon freshly ground nutmeg
    (or to taste)
¼   teaspoon freshly grated lemon rind
2   egg yolks, beaten
¼   cup heavy cream

GENEROUSLY BUTTER A 2-QUART casserole or baking dish and set aside.

■ *Preheat oven to 325°F.*

Wash and drain rice well. Combine rice with milk, sugar, salt, vanilla, nutmeg, and lemon rind. Pour into prepared casserole and place in a baking pan filled with water that comes 1 inch up the sides. Place in preheated oven and bake for about 2 hours, stirring at least three times during the first hour to prevent rice from clumping and sticking to the bottom.

Combine egg yolks and heavy cream until well blended. After 1½ hours of baking, quickly stir egg mixture into rice. Bake for an additional 30 minutes or until rice is cooked and pudding is light-brown and set. Serve warm or at room temperature.

Combine egg yolks and heavy cream until well blended. After 1½ hours of baking, quickly stir egg mixture into rice. Bake for an additional 30 minutes or until rice is cooked and pudding is light-brown and set. Serve warm or at room temperature.

VARIATIONS:
1. Add ½ cup raisins and ½ teaspoon cinnamon when adding eggs.
2. Add ¾ cup unsweetened coconut when adding eggs.
3. Add 1 cup chopped mixed dried fruit when adding eggs.

BERRY/FRUIT COBBLER

Serves 6 to 8.

YOU CAN MAKE A COBBLER FROM ANY fruit or any combination of fruits. The most traditional are cherry, peach, and blueberry.

3 to 4 cups washed, peeled, cored
     or pitted berries or fruit
1   cup sugar (or to taste)
1   large egg, beaten
2   tablespoons cornstarch
1   teaspoon ground cinnamon
    (optional)
1   teaspoon fresh lemon juice
    Sweet Biscuit Dough*
    Cinnamon Sugar*

■ *Preheat oven to 400°F.*

GENEROUSLY BUTTER A 2-QUART casserole or a 9-inch-square baking dish. Combine fruit and sugar. When sugar has begun to dissolve, stir in egg, cornstarch, cinnamon, and lemon juice. When combined, pour into prepared pan.

Drop Sweet Biscuit Dough on top of the fruit by tablespoonfuls. When top is generously covered, sprinkle with Cinnamon Sugar and place in preheated oven. Bake for about 30 minutes or until top is lightly browned and fruit is bubbling. Serve warm with heavy cream, Vanilla Ice Cream*, whipped cream, or any light dessert sauce.

SWEET BISCUIT DOUGH

Makes enough for 1 cobbler or at least 12 shortcake biscuits.

2   cups all-purpose flour
4   teaspoons baking powder
3   tablespoons sugar
½   cup chilled butter or solid
    vegetable shortening
¾   cup milk

PLACE DRY INGREDIENTS IN FOOD processor fitted with the metal blade. Cut in butter using quick on-and-off turns. When crumbly, pour in milk and process quickly into a soft dough. Roll out to ½-inch thickness on a lightly floured board, and cut into biscuit rounds, or drop by the spoonful, depending upon the recipe requirement.

If making shortcake biscuits, preheat oven to 450°F. Place biscuits close to one another in a round cake pan. Place in preheated oven and bake for about 15 minutes or until golden-brown.

CINNAMON SUGAR

Makes about ½ cup.

CINNAMON SUGAR IS GREAT TO KEEP on hand for toast or to sprinkle on cakes or pies.

½   cup superfine sugar
1½   teaspoons freshly ground
    cinnamon

COMBINE SUGAR AND CINNAMON AND store, covered, in a cool, dark place.

Peaches and blackberries make a luscious Fruit Cobbler, here topped with sweet whipped cream.

FRESH COCONUT CAKE

▬▬ *Makes one 9-inch 3-layer cake.*

1 fresh coconut
4 large eggs
1 cup unsalted butter
1½ cups sugar
2 teaspoons pure vanilla extract
2⅔ cups unleavened cake flour
1½ teaspoons baking powder
½ cup milk
   Lemon Filling*
2 cups freshly grated coconut
   Coconut Icing*

■ *Preheat oven to 350°F.*

GRATE THE WHITE MEAT OF ONE FRESH coconut. Place in a heat-proof bowl and cover with boiling water. Let steep for 1 hour. Strain liquid through a very fine sieve or cheese-cloth. Discard coconut meat. You should have at least 1 cup coconut milk. Set aside ½ cup of milk and reserve remaining for Coconut Icing.

Butter and flour three 9-inch-round layer cake pans and set aside.

Separate eggs. Beat whites until stiff but not dry and set aside.

Cream butter and sugar until light and fluffy. Add egg yolks and vanilla to creamed mixture and stir to combine.

Resift cake flour with baking powder. Combine coconut milk and milk and add to creamed mixture

alternately with sifted flour and baking powder. When well combined, fold in egg whites.

Pour equal portions into each of the three prepared pans. Place in preheated oven and bake for 25 minutes or until cake tester inserted in center comes out clean. Remove from pans and cool on wire cake racks.

When cool, place one layer on cake plate; cover with Lemon Filling and sprinkle with freshly grated coconut. Top with another layer of cake, cover with Lemon Filling, and sprinkle with coconut. Top with final layer of cake, holding layers in place with toothpicks if necessary. Generously cover entire cake with Coconut Icing and cover the whole cake with the remaining grated coconut. Do not refrigerate.

LEMON FILLING

*Makes enough to fill
one 9-inch cake.*

1   tablespoon plus 1 teaspoon
    cornstarch
1   cup superfine sugar
3   large eggs
¼   cup fresh lemon juice
½   teaspoon finely grated lemon rind
2   tablespoons unsalted butter

COMBINE CORNSTARCH AND SUGAR.
Stir in with eggs, lemon juice, and
rind in a small, heavy saucepan
over low heat. Cook, stirring constantly, for about 10 minutes or
until slightly thick. Whisk in butter
and continue cooking until very
thick. Remove from heat and set
aside to cool. The filling may be
made in advance and stored, covered and refrigerated, for up to one
day.

COCONUT ICING

*Makes enough to frost
one 9-inch cake.*

2   large egg whites
1½ cups superfine sugar
2   tablespoons cold coconut milk
¼   teaspoon cream of tartar
1   teaspoon white Karo® syrup
1   teaspoon pure vanilla extract

COMBINE ALL INGREDIENTS IN THE
top half of double boiler over boiling
water. Beat, using a hand-held electric mixer, for 6 minutes or until
fluffy and able to hold peaks.
    Remove from heat and use im-
mediately.

STRAWBERRY SHORTCAKE

Serves 8.

1   recipe Sweet Biscuit Dough*
4   cups sliced fresh strawberries
½   cup sugar (or to taste)
½   teaspoon grated fresh orange rind
    Chantilly Cream*

PREPARE SWEET BISCUIT DOUGH AND
bake as for shortcake biscuits, as
directed on page 105. When baked,
split biscuits in half.
    Combine strawberries, sugar,
and orange rind and use a fork to
slightly mash some of the berries.
Let stand for 15 minutes.
    Place one to two biscuits, de-
pending on size, on each of eight
serving plates. Open the halves and
place a generous portion of strawberries on top of the bottom half. Place
top half over berries, drizzle additional berries on top, and place a
generous portion of Chantilly
Cream* on top. Serve immediately.

ANGEL FOOD CAKE

Makes 1 tube cake.

THIS IS THE PERFECT LOW-cholesterol, no-fat dessert. If you follow the directions exactly and work quickly, you will make the lightest Angel Food Cake you've ever tasted.

1 cup sifted cake flour
1½ cups sifted superfine sugar
1½ cups egg whites, at room temperature (about 13 eggs)
¼ teaspoon salt
1½ teaspoons cream of tartar
1 teaspoon pure vanilla extract

■ *Preheat oven to 375°F.*

SIFT TOGETHER THE SIFTED CAKE flour with half of the sifted sugar at least three times. Using an electric mixer, beat the egg whites and salt until foamy. Sprinkle in cream of tartar and beat until soft peaks form. (This is important. The egg whites should have a dull finish and the peaks should hold, but not be firm and sharp.)

Slowly sprinkle sugar over egg whites, beating slowly to incorporate. Using the slower speed, fold in the flour-sugar mixture one-third at a time, scraping sides and bottom of the bowl after each incorporation.

Immediately pour into a clean, ungreased angel food cake pan with removable bottom. Cut the batter with a kitchen knife to release air bubbles. Place in preheated oven and bake for about 35 minutes, or until golden-brown and a cake tester inserted in the center comes out clean. Do not open oven door for the first 20 minutes or the cake might fall.

When cake is done, remove from oven. If pan has feet, turn upside down. If not, invert it by placing tube hole over the neck of a heat-proof bottle. Allow to cool for at least two hours. When completely cooled, turn cake right side up and carefully and gently run a sharp knife around the edges and lift cake from pan, holding on to the tube. Slowly and carefully run knife around tube and between cake and bottom. Invert cake onto cake plate and tap it free. Sprinkle with 2 tablespoons confectioner's sugar, if desired.

NOTE: Angel Food Cake is delicious served with fresh fruit and heavy cream. If you want to frost it, use only a very light frosting, such as whipped cream.

CHOCOLATE CREAM PIE

Serves 6 to 8.

½   pastry recipe for fruit pies (see page 111)
1   recipe Chocolate Pudding*
1   cup heavy cream
1   tablespoon confectioner's sugar
½   teaspoon pure vanilla extract
1   tablespoon chocolate sprinkles or chocolate shavings

■ *Preheat oven to 450°F.*

ROLL OUT PASTRY AS DIRECTED ON page 114. Place in a 9-inch pie pan. Press into pan and crimp edges using your thumb and forefinger. Place a piece of parchment paper or aluminum foil over pastry and line with dried beans, rice, or a pastry weight. Place in preheated oven and bake for 25 minutes or until pastry is cooked and edges are light-brown.

Remove from oven and let stand for 5 minutes. Remove lining and weights.

Pour cooled chocolate pudding into baked pie shell. Whip cream with sugar and vanilla until it reaches stiff peaks. Cover chocolate pudding with whipped cream. Sprinkle top with chocolate sprinkles or shavings. Refrigerate until ready to serve.

CHOCOLATE PUDDING

Serves 6.

⅓   cup cocoa
¾   cup sugar (or to taste)
¼   cup cornstarch
2   cups half-and-half
1   large egg yolk
1   teaspoon pure vanilla extract

COMBINE COCOA, SUGAR, AND CORN-starch.

Heat half-and-half in a medium-sized saucepan over medium heat for about 4 minutes or just until bubbles begin to form around the edges. Whisk in chocolate mixture until well blended. Stir a bit of the chocolate into the egg yolk, then whisk the egg yolk into the choco-late. Cook, whisking constantly, for

about 4 minutes or until pudding is thick. Remove from heat and pour into individual dessert dishes or into a heat-proof serving bowl. Cover tops with wax paper or plastic wrap to prevent hardening. Let cool to room temperature, then refrigerate if necessary. Remove wax paper and serve as is or with whipped cream.

DEVIL'S FLOAT

Serves 6 to 8.

AS UNBELIEVABLE AS IT MIGHT SEEM, my mother made the marshmallows that this recipe requires. I don't have her patience, so I just buy a bag of those campfire favorites.

2 tablespoons unsalted butter
1 cup sugar
1 teaspoon pure vanilla extract
1 cup all-purpose flour
1 teaspoon baking powder
⅓ cup cocoa
½ cup milk
½ cup walnut or pecan pieces
1½ cups water
12 large marshmallows

CREAM BUTTER AND ½ CUP SUGAR until light yellow. Stir in vanilla. Sift the flour, baking powder, and cocoa together, then add to the butter mixture alternately with the milk until well blended. Set aside.

■ *Preheat oven to 350°F.*

Place water and remaining sugar in a saucepan over medium heat. Bring to a boil and boil for 5 minutes. Pour into a 1½-quart casserole. Lay marshmallows on top. Drop chocolate batter over syrup-marshmallow mixture by the tablespoonful. Place in preheated oven and bake for 45 minutes or until cake tester inserted in the center comes out clean. Serve warm with whipped cream, Chantilly Cream*, or Vanilla Ice Cream*, if desired.

BREAD PUDDING

Serves 6 to 8.

1 tablespoon unsalted butter
3 cups hot milk
3 large eggs, beaten
⅔ cup light brown sugar (or to taste)
2 tablespoons melted unsalted butter
1 teaspoon pure vanilla extract
Pinch salt
3 cups stale French bread cubes
½ cup chopped walnuts or pecans

■ *Preheat oven to 350°F.*

GENEROUSLY BUTTER AN 8-INCH-square baking dish.
Combine milk, eggs, brown sugar, melted butter, vanilla, and salt. Place bread cubes in prepared dish. Sprinkle with nuts. Pour milk mixture over top and place in another dish filled with hot water that comes 1 inch up the sides. Place in preheated oven and bake for 35 minutes or until golden-brown and puffed. Serve hot with Chantilly Cream*.

CUSTARD

Serves 6.

2   large eggs
3   tablespoons sugar
    Pinch salt
2   cups milk
1   teaspoon pure vanilla extract
    Freshly ground nutmeg to taste
    (optional)

■ *Preheat oven to 300°F.*

BEAT THE EGGS, SUGAR, AND SALT until very light.

Heat milk in a medium-sized saucepan over medium heat for about 4 minutes or just until bubbles begin to form around the edges. Immediately whisk into eggs. Stir in vanilla and nutmeg.

Pour into six individual custard cups or one 1-quart ovenproof serving dish. Set cups in a baking pan with hot water that comes ½ inch up the sides. Place in preheated oven and bake for about 15 minutes or until custards are firm in the center. Serve warm or at room temperature.

VARIATION:
Place 1 tablespoon brown sugar in bottom of each custard cup, or ½ cup in bottom of the larger dish. Place in preheated 300°F oven until melted. Swirl melted sugar around the inside of the custard cup, then immediately fill with custard and bake as above.

FLOATING ISLAND

Serves 6 to 8.

5   large eggs
¾   cup sugar
3   cups milk
1½ teaspoons pure vanilla extract

SEPARATE THREE OF THE EGGS. BEAT the three egg whites until soft peaks form. Slowly add ¼ cup sugar and beat until stiff.

Heat milk in a heavy 10-inch skillet over medium heat for about 4 minutes or until bubbles form around the edges. Drop six to eight mounds of egg whites into milk. Simmer for about 5 minutes or until meringues are set. Use a slotted spoon to lift meringues from milk. Drain on paper towels. When well drained, place on a plate and refrigerate.

Pour milk into a medium-sized saucepan. Beat egg yolks with remaining eggs and sugar. When combined, whisk into milk. Place over medium heat and cook, stirring constantly, for about 10 minutes or until custard coats the back of a spoon. Stir in vanilla. Place in a pan of cold water and stir frequently to slightly chill. Pour into a serving bowl and cover with a piece of wax paper and refrigerate.

When chilled, top with meringues and serve immediately.

BASIC CUPCAKES

■■■■ *Makes approximately 18 cupcakes.*

THIS IS A SIMPLE, QUICK DESSERT. However, any cake batter may be used to make cupcakes. For convenience, use disposable paper baking cups or seasoned muffin tins coated with a nonstick spray. When using a cake recipe, baking time at 350°F should be about 20 minutes.

¼	cup unsalted butter or margarine
1	cup sugar
1	teaspoon pure vanilla extract
1	large egg
2	cups all-purpose flour (or 1⅔ cups all-purpose flour and ⅓ cup cocoa for chocolate batter)
3	teaspoons baking powder
	Pinch salt
¾	cup milk

■ *Preheat oven to 350°F.*

CREAM BUTTER AND SUGAR AND VA-nilla until light and fluffy. Beat in egg. Sift dry ingredients together and alternately add to butter mixture with milk. Pour into lined or seasoned muffin tins in a preheated oven. Bake for 20 minutes or until a cake tester inserted in the center comes out clean.

Serve as is, sprinkled with confectioner's sugar, or cover with any frosting.

VARIATION:
Carefully cut top off cupcake and cut out a small hole in the center. Fill with whipped cream or commercially prepared marshmallow cream. Put top back on cupcake. Cover with any frosting.

An assortment of Cupcakes, frosted with vanilla, chocolate, and strawberry butter cream and topped with coconut shavings and colored sprinkles. Something for everyone and perfect for parties.

FRUIT PIES

▬

Serves 6 to 8.

I MADE PIES EVERY DAY FOR ALMOST ten years and I still think that there is no dessert more American than a hot fruit pie with homemade vanilla ice cream.

▬

*Makes pastry for one
9-inch, 2-crust pie.*

2   cups sifted all-purpose flour
¼   teaspoon salt
⅔   cup chilled solid vegetable
     shortening
     Approximately ¼ cup ice water
     Fruit Filling*
     Approximately 2 tablespoons
     unsalted butter
     Vanilla Ice Cream*

■ *Preheat oven to 450°F.*

COMBINE FLOUR AND SALT IN FOOD processor fitted with the metal blade. Cut in shortening using quick on-and-off turns until crumbly. Add water, 1 tablespoon at a time, until dough comes together in a ball. Do not overmix or get too wet.

Remove from processor. Wrap in plastic wrap and refrigerate for 15 minutes to chill slightly. Remove from refrigerator and divide dough in half. Roll out to ½- to ⅛-inch thickness on a lightly floured board.

Line the bottom of a 9-inch pie pan leaving edges overlapping. Roll out remaining half to ¼-inch thickness and set aside. Fill pie pan with desired Fruit Filling. Dot with butter. Place remaining pastry circle on top, pressing edges of the two pastries together with your thumb and forefinger. Trim off excess pastry. Use a sharp knife to cut air vents in top of the pie in a decorative pattern.

Place in preheated oven and bake for 20 minutes. Reduce heat to 350°F and bake for an additional 20 minutes or until pastry is golden-brown and fruit is bubbling. Remove from heat and allow to cool on a wire rack for at least 15 minutes before cutting.

FRUIT FILLINGS

Makes one 9-inch pie.

APPLE: Toss together

6 to 8 Granny Smith or other tart cooking apples, peeled, cored, and sliced
½ teaspoon fresh lemon juice
1 teaspoon ground cinnamon
  Nutmeg to taste
¾ cup sugar (or to taste)
2 tablespoons all-purpose flour
1 teaspoon melted unsalted butter
2 tablespoons apple cider (optional) (you can also add 1 cup chopped nuts and/or ½ cup raisins or use 6 apples and 1 cup chopped dried fruit or 1 cup fresh cranberries)

SOUR CHERRY, ANY BERRY, PEACH, Apricot, Rhubarb, or other fruit: Toss together

4 cups pitted, peeled, and sliced (if necessary) fruit
1½ teaspoons quick-cooking tapioca or 2 tablespoons cornstarch
1 cup sugar (or to taste, depending on fruit)
1 tablespoon fresh lemon juice
  Dash nutmeg or cinnamon (optional)

VANILLA ICE CREAM

Makes approximately 1 quart.

2 cups milk
2 large eggs plus 1 large egg yolk
¾ cup sugar
2 tablespoons pure vanilla extract
½ teaspoon finely grated vanilla bean
2 cups heavy cream

HEAT MILK OVER MEDIUM HEAT FOR 4 minutes or just until bubbles form around the edges. Remove from heat.

Beat eggs, egg yolk, and sugar until light. Slowly pour in hot milk, beating constantly. Return to pan and cook, stirring constantly over low heat, for about 10 minutes or until thick. Remove from heat and allow to cool.

When cool, whisk in vanilla, vanilla bean, and cream. Using an electric ice cream freezer, freeze and store according to manufacturer's directions.

BROWNIES

▬ *Makes approximately 2 dozen brownies.*

3   ounces solid unsweetened chocolate
⅓   cup unsalted butter
2   large eggs
½   cup white sugar
½   cup light brown sugar
1   teaspoon pure vanilla extract
¾   cup all-purpose flour
½   teaspoon baking powder
¼   teaspoon salt (optional)
1   cup chopped walnuts or pecans

■ *Preheat oven to 350°F.*

GREASE AND FLOUR A 9-INCH-SQUARE baking pan.

Place chocolate and butter in top half of double boiler over boiling water. Stir constantly until melted and combined.

Beat eggs until light. Add sugars and vanilla and beat until well combined. Add chocolate and butter mixture and beat until very well combined.

Sift together flour, baking powder, and salt, then stir into chocolate mixture until just combined. Add walnuts and stir. Pour into prepared pan and place in preheated oven. Bake for about 25 minutes or until top is dry and the edges are beginning to come away from the pan. Brownies should not be firm.

Remove from oven and place on a wire rack to cool for at least 30 minutes before cutting.

LEMON MERINGUE PIE

▬ *Makes one 9-inch pie.*

1½   cups sugar
2   tablespoons cornstarch
2   tablespoons all-purpose flour
⅛   teaspoon salt
1¾   cups water
     Juice and freshly grated rind of 1 lemon
3   egg yolks
¼   cup unsalted butter, cut into bits
1   teaspoon pure vanilla extract
1   baked pastry shell
     Never-Fail Meringue*

■ *Preheat oven to 400°F.*

COMBINE THE SUGAR, CORNSTARCH, flour, and salt in a saucepan. Whisk in water and place over medium heat. Cook, stirring constantly, for about 5 minutes or until thick. Stir in lemon juice and rind.

Mix a bit of the warm lemon mixture into the egg yolks, then whisk eggs into the remaining lemon mixture in saucepan. Beat in butter and vanilla and whisk until well blended and thick.

Pour into prepared pie shell. Cover with Never-Fail Meringue and place in preheated oven and bake for 10 minutes or until meringue is golden-brown.

NEVER-FAIL MERINGUE

■ *Makes enough for one 9-inch pie.*

½ cup water
1 tablespoon cornstarch dissolved in
   1 tablespoon water
3 egg whites
6 tablespoons superfine sugar

PLACE THE WATER IN A SMALL SAUCE-pan over high heat and bring to a boil. When boiling, whisk in dissolved cornstarch and cook, stirring constantly, until water is clear. Remove from heat and cool.

With electric mixer set at the lowest speed, beat egg whites in a large bowl. Increase speed and alternately add the cooled liquid and sugar to the egg whites, beating until stiff and shiny. Place a large amount of the meringue on top of the center of a filled pie shell. Put small spoonfuls of meringue around the edge of the shell. Spread from the center out to meet the edge, being sure that the entire top is covered and edges are sealed. Bake as directed.

SCHAUM TORTE

■ *Serves 8 to 10.*

MY OLDEST FRIEND, HU, TAUGHT ME to make his favorite dessert.

6 large egg whites
2 cups superfine sugar
⅛ teaspoon baking powder
¼ teaspoon salt
1 teaspoon pure vanilla extract
1 tablespoon white vinegar
3 cups sliced fresh fruit or berries
1 cup heavy cream, whipped

■ *Preheat oven to 250°F.*

BEAT EGG WHITES UNTIL FOAMY. Slowly add sugar and beat until almost stiff. Add baking powder, salt, vanilla, and vinegar and beat until stiff and glossy.

Line a baking sheet with parchment or wax paper. Mound the meringue in the center and spread out to make a 9-inch circle. Place in preheated oven and bake for 1 hour. Turn off heat and allow to cool in the oven. Do not open door.

When cool, remove from oven and place on serving plate. Cut about ½ inch off the top. Cover with fruit. Top with whipped cream, then break top into pieces and place in the cream. Place in refrigerator for 1 hour before serving.

OATMEAL COOKIES

Makes about 5 dozen.

1½ cups all-purpose flour
1¾ cups uncooked oatmeal (not instant)
1   teaspoon ground cinnamon
¼   teaspoon ground allspice
     Dash ground cloves
¼   teaspoon salt
½   teaspoon baking soda
½   teaspoon baking powder
½   cup unsalted butter
¾   cup light brown sugar
2   large eggs
1   teaspoon pure vanilla extract
5   tablespoons milk
1   cup raisins
1   cup cooked walnuts or pecans

■ *Preheat oven to 350°F.*

COMBINE FLOUR, OATMEAL, CINNA-mon, allspice, cloves, salt, baking soda, and baking powder and set aside.

Beat butter and sugar until creamy. Add eggs and vanilla. Stir until well combined. Add milk. Stir in dry ingredients. When well combined, stir in raisins and nuts.

Drop by the teaspoonful onto greased cookie sheets. Place in pre-heated oven and bake for 10 min-utes or until light-brown. Remove from oven and lift cookies onto wire racks to cool.

CHOCOLATE-CHIP COOKIES

Makes approximately 4 dozen cookies.

½   cup unsalted butter
¼   cup white sugar
½   cup light brown sugar
1   large egg
1   teaspoon pure vanilla extract
1¼   cups all-purpose flour
½   teaspoon baking soda
¼   teaspoon baking powder
1½   cups chocolate bits
¾   cup walnut pieces (optional)

■ *Preheat oven to 375°F.*

CREAM BUTTER AND SUGARS UNTIL light and fluffy. Beat in egg and vanilla. When well combined, stir in flour, baking soda, and baking powder. Add chocolate bits and nuts. Drop by the teaspoonful onto ungreased cookie sheets.

Place in preheated oven and bake for 10 minutes or until just soft. Remove from oven and lift cookies onto wire racks to cool.

VARIATIONS:
1. Replace ¼ cup flour with ¼ cup cocoa for Chocolate Chocolate-Chip Cookies.
2. Add ¾ cup unsweetened coconut flakes and/or ½ cup raisins to the basic recipe.

SUGAR COOKIES

Makes approximately 5 dozen cookies.

1   cup unsalted butter
2   cups sugar
2   teaspoons pure vanilla extract
2   large egg yolks
4   cups sifted all-purpose flour
4   teaspoons baking powder
¼   cup milk

CREAM BUTTER AND SUGAR UNTIL light and fluffy. Add vanilla and egg yolks and beat to combine.

Sift flour and baking powder together and add to cream mixture alternately with milk. When well combined, form into a log at least 2½ inches in diameter. Wrap in wax paper and chill for at least 2 hours.

■ *Preheat oven to 375°F.*

When ready to bake, slice about ⅛-inch thick and place 2 inches apart on lightly greased cookie sheets. Place in preheated oven and bake for 10 minutes or until edges are lightly browned and cookie centers are done.

NOTE: You can also sprinkle the cookies with plain sugar or Cinnamon Sugar* before baking.

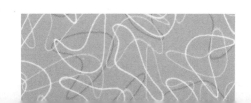

NECESSITIES

MEASUREMENTS AND ABBREVIATIONS

KITCHEN METRICS

SUBSTITUTIONS

COOKING TERMS AND TIMES

COOKING CHARTS

7

FROM A
COOK'S
DIARY

NECESSITIES

WHEN PURCHASING KITCHEN EQUIP-
ment it is always best to buy the
best quality possible. Invest in
heavy-duty pots and pans with
tight-fitting lids, fine quality nonstick baking pans, properly sized
frying and sauté pans for ease of
handling, professional quality elec-
trical appliances, stainless steel and
Pyrex bowls, and the finest knives
available. If you do so, your kitchen
will be stocked for your entire cooking life.

Besides quality equipment,
every kitchen should have some
basic ingredients on hand at all
times. Flours, sugars, leavening
agents, eggs, cheeses, rices, pastas,
canned tomatoes, dried fruits and
beans, smoked meats, dried and
fresh herbs, onions, garlic, and nuts
are some of the stores you should
always find on your shelves. Your
freezer should always contain a
supply of meat, chicken, vegetable,
and fish stocks as well as some clarified butter. The recipes for these
follow.

MEAT OR CHICKEN STOCK

▬▬ *Makes approximately 2 quarts.*

2   pounds shinbones, cracked
1   large knuckle bone
1   pound lean meat
    or
6   pounds chicken necks, backs,
    and wings
1   large onion, peeled and studded
    with 2 cloves
2   leeks, washed and chopped
1   large carrot, washed and
    chopped
2   stalks celery, washed and chopped
2   tablespoons minced fresh parsley
1   teaspoon minced fresh thyme
1   teaspoon whole peppercorns
    Salt to taste
    Approximately 4 quarts cold water

■ *Preheat oven to 400°F.*

PLACE BONES AND MEAT ON A BAKING
sheet with sides in a preheated oven.
Bake for about 20 minutes (15 minutes for chicken) or until brown
and some fat has rendered out.

Place remaining ingredients in a
large stockpot with 4 quarts cold
water over high heat. Bring to a
boil and add browned bones and
meat. Again bring to a boil. When
boiling, lower heat to a simmer and
simmer for about 3½ hours, skimming off the scum as the broth
cooks. Remove from heat and let
rest for 30 minutes.

Line a colander with cheesecloth
or a double layer of paper towels.
Drain broth through it and discard
bones and vegetables. Re-strain
stock through a fine sieve. Allow
stock to cool before refrigerating or
freezing. When cool, skim off fat.
Store covered in small containers,
from 1 to 2 cups. The stock can be
refrigerated for up to three days or
tightly sealed and frozen for up to
six months.

VEGETABLE STOCK

▬▬ *Makes approximately 2 quarts.*

2   onions, peeled and chopped
2   carrots, washed and chopped
2   potatoes, washed and chopped
2   leeks, washed and chopped
4   stalks celery, washed and chopped
¼   pound mushrooms, wiped clean and chopped
1   tomato, washed, cored, and chopped
1   artichoke, washed and quartered
2   teaspoons minced fresh parsley
½   teaspoon peppercorns
    Salt to taste
3½ quarts cold water

COMBINE ALL INGREDIENTS IN A heavy stockpot over high heat. Bring to a boil. When boiling, lower heat to a simmer. Simmer for 2 hours.

Line a colander with cheesecloth or a double layer of paper towels. Drain broth through it and discard vegetables. Restrain stock through a fine sieve. Allow stock to cool before refrigerating or freezing. Store covered in small containers, from 1 to 2 cups. The stock can be refrigerated for up to three days or tightly sealed and frozen for up to six months.

FISH STOCK

▬▬ *Makes approximately 2 quarts.*

5   pounds fish bones from nonoily fish such as flounder, sole, halibut, and shrimp and/or lobster shells
2   leeks, washed and chopped
3   shallots, peeled and chopped
1   small onion, peeled and chopped
1   carrot, peeled and chopped
1   cup dry white wine
2   tablespoons fresh lemon juice
1   tablespoon minced fresh parsley
1   bay leaf
½   teaspoon white peppercorns
    Salt to taste
3   quarts cold water

WASH BONES WELL. PLACE IN A stockpot with remaining ingredients over high heat. Bring to a boil. When boiling, lower heat to a simmer. Simmer for 1½ hours.

Line a colander with cheesecloth or a double layer of paper towels. Drain broth through it and discard bones, vegetables, and bay leaf. Restrain stock through a fine sieve. Allow stock to cool before refrigerating or freezing. When cool, skim off any fat. Store covered in small containers, from 1 to 2 cups. The stock can be refrigerated for up to two days or tightly sealed and frozen for up to six months.

CLARIFIED BUTTER

▬▬ *Makes approximately 1½ cups.*

CLARIFIED BUTTER DOES NOT BURN as readily as whole butter. It is therefore perfect for sautéeing or searing.

1   pound unsalted butter

MELT BUTTER IN A MEDIUM-SIZED saucepan over very low heat. Keep over low heat for approximately 20 minutes, skimming off the white froth as it forms. Raise heat slightly and continue to skim off white matter until remaining butter is clear. This should take about 30 minutes. Do not allow butter to simmer or boil.

Remove from heat and let stand 15 minutes. Skim off any particles that form. Carefully pour clarified butter into storage containers, discarding the watery bottom. Store either covered and refrigerated for up to one week or tightly sealed and frozen for up to three months.

ABBREVIATIONS

t	=	TEASPOON
T	=	TABLESPOON
c	=	CUP
#	=	POUND

MEASUREMENTS

	PINCH	= 2 DROPS	
	DASH	= 6 DROPS	
1/2	OUNCE	= 1 TABLESPOON	= 3 TEASPOONS
1	OUNCE	= 2 TABLESPOONS	= 1/8 CUP
2	OUNCES	= 4 TABLESPOONS	= 1/4 CUP
5	TABLESPOONS	+ 1 TEASPOON	= 1/3 CUP
4	OUNCES	= 8 TABLESPOONS	= 1/2 CUP
8	OUNCES	= 1 CUP = 16 TABLESPOONS	= 1/2 PINT
16	OUNCES	= 2 CUPS	= 1 PINT
32	OUNCES	= 4 CUPS	= 1 QUART
4	QUARTS	= 16 CUPS	= 1 GALLON
1	POUND	= 16 OUNCES	
1	POUND FLOUR	= 3 1/2 CUPS	
1	POUND GRANULATED OR BROWN SUGAR	= 2 1/4 CUPS	
1	POUND CONFECTIONER'S SUGAR	= 2 3/4 CUPS	
5	LARGE EGGS	= 1 CUP	
8	LARGE EGG WHITES	= 1 CUP	
16	LARGE EGG YOLKS	= 1 CUP	
1	POUND BUTTER	= 2 CUPS	
1	CUP HEAVY CREAM	= 2 CUPS WHIPPED CREAM	
1	POUND HARD CHEESE	= APPROXIMATELY 4 CUPS GRATED CHEESE	
1	POUND RICE	= 2 CUPS UNCOOKED OR APPROXIMATELY 7 CUPS COOKED	
1	POUND DRIED PASTA	= APPROXIMATELY 8 TO 9 CUPS COOKED	
1	POUND DRIED BEANS	= APPROXIMATELY 2 CUPS UNCOOKED OR 6 CUPS COOKED	
1	POUND POTATOES	= APPROXIMATELY 3 1/2 CUPS COOKED	
1	LEMON	= APPROXIMATELY 2 1/2 TABLESPOONS JUICE OR 1 TEASPOON GRATED RIND	
1	APPLE	= APPROXIMATELY 1 CUP SLICED	
1	ONION	= APPROXIMATELY 1/2 CUP DICED	
1	CLOVE GARLIC	= APPROXIMATELY 1 TEASPOON MINCED	
1	BELL PEPPER	= APPROXIMATELY 1 CUP DICED	
1	TABLESPOON MINCED FRESH HERBS	= 1 TEASPOON DRIED	
1	TABLESPOON PREPARED MUSTARD	= 1 TEASPOON DRIED	

SUBSTITUTIONS

BAKING POWDER:
1/4 teaspoon baking soda plus 1/2 cup sour milk or buttermilk or yogurt. Reduce liquid in recipe by 1/2 cup.

1 OUNCE SOLID UNSWEETENED CHOCOLATE:
1 tablespoon unsalted butter plus 3 tablespoons cocoa powder

FLOUR AS A THICKENING AGENT:
For every tablespoon:
1 teaspoon arrowroot or potato flour or
2 teaspoons cornstarch or
2 teaspoons quick-cooking tapioca.

SUGAR—PER CUP:
1 cup honey less 1/4 cup of the liquid called for in recipe.

WHOLE MILK:
1/2 cup evaporated milk plus 1/2 cup water, or
1/4 cup dry milk reconstituted in 1 cup water plus
1 teaspoon unsalted butter.

SOUR MILK—PER CUP:
1 cup whole milk plus
1 teaspoon vinegar or lemon juice

COOKING TERMS AND TIMES

TO BOIL is to cook in water or another liquid that has reached 212°F on a food thermometer.

TO STEW is to cook in liquid over low heat on top of the stove for a long period of time.

TO BLANCH is to immerse in boiling water for seconds or at the most 2 minutes to set color and crispness, to make a fruit or vegetable easy to peel, or to slightly cook tender foods.

TO SHOCK is to set blanched foods in ice water or cold running water.

TO SAUTÉ is to cook, stirring constantly, in a small amount of fat over medium heat on top of the stove. (You may also shake the pan vigorously to sauté.)

TO SEAR is to quickly brown meats in very hot fat over high heat on top of the stove.

TO FRY is to cook in fat, usually in a heavy skillet at fairly high heat, on top of the stove.

TO DEEP-FAT FRY is to cook by immersion in a large quantity of fat heated to 365°F on a food thermometer.

TO BAKE is to cook in an oven.

TO ROAST is to bake meat in an oven.

TO BROIL is to cook under an open flame in an enclosed gas or electric stove.

TO GRILL is to cook on a rack over an open flame or hot coals.

TO BARBECUE is to grill with the addition of a sauce.

KITCHEN METRICS

FOR COOKING AND BAKING CONVENIENCE, THE METRIC COMMISSION OF CANADA SUGGESTS THE FOLLOWING FOR ADAPTING TO METRIC MEASUREMENT. THE TABLE GIVES APPROXIMATE, RATHER THAN EXACT, CONVERSIONS.

SPOONS

1/4 TEASPOON	= 1 MILLILITER
1/2 TEASPOON	= 2 MILLILITERS
1 TEASPOON	= 5 MILLILITERS
1 TABLESPOON	= 15 MILLILITERS
2 TABLESPOONS	= 25 MILLILITERS
3 TABLESPOONS	= 50 MILLILITERS

CUPS

1/4 CUP	= 50 MILLILITERS
1/3 CUP	= 75 MILLILITERS
1/2 CUP	= 125 MILLILITERS
2/3 CUP	= 150 MILLILITERS
3/4 CUP	= 175 MILLILITERS
1 CUP	= 250 MILLILITERS

OVEN TEMPERATURES

200°F	= 100°C	350°F	= 180°C
225°F	= 110°C	375°F	= 190°C
250°F	= 120°C	400°F	= 200°C
275°F	= 140°C	425°F	= 220°C
300°F	= 150°C	450°F	= 230°C
325°F	= 160°C	475°F	= 240°C

COOKING CHARTS

THE TEMPERATURES LISTED BELOW ARE IN ACCORDANCE WITH THOSE FOUND ON A MEAT THERMOMETER. TRADITIONALLY, THE USDA CONSIDERS 160°F RARE.

ROASTING BEEF

140°F RARE	APPROXIMATELY 20 MINUTES PER POUND
160°F MEDIUM	APPROXIMATELY 23 MINUTES PER POUND
170°F WELL DONE	APPROXIMATELY 26 MINUTES PER POUND

ROASTING VEAL

140°F RARE	APPROXIMATELY 15 MINUTES PER POUND
150°F MEDIUM	APPROXIMATELY 18 MINUTES PER POUND
170°F WELL DONE	APPROXIMATELY 23 MINUTES PER POUND

ROASTING LAMB

145°F RARE	APPROXIMATELY 20 MINUTES PER POUND
160°F MEDIUM	APPROXIMATELY 22 MINUTES PER POUND
175°F WELL DONE	APPROXIMATELY 26 MINUTES PER POUND

1-INCH-THICK LAMB CHOPS BROILED/PAN-BROILED

FOR RARE	APPROXIMATELY 4 MINUTES PER SIDE
FOR MEDIUM	APPROXIMATELY 6 MINUTES PER SIDE

ROASTING PORK

THERE IS SOME DEBATE ABOUT WHETHER PORK STILL HAS TO BE SERVED WELL DONE TO ELIMINATE THE POSSIBILITY OF TRICHINOSIS. I STILL SERVE PORK WELL DONE, WHICH IS 185°F ON A MEAT THERMOMETER.

1-INCH-THICK PORK CHOPS BROILED/PAN-BROILED

APPROXIMATELY 18 MINUTES PER SIDE

INDEX